Copyright © 2014 by Ehud Segev

All rights reserved. Except as permitted under the U.S. Copyright Act of 1976, no part of this publication may be reproduced, distributed, or transmitted in any form or by any means, or stores in a database or retrieval system, without the prior written permission of the publisher.

Published by MENTALIZER™, CORP.
Mentalizer Education.
450 West 58th Street, Suite 1H
New York, NY 10019
Visit our Web site at www.mentalizer.com

Originally published in hardcover by CreateSpace, September 2013.
First Edition: September 2013.
Second Edition: November 2013.
Third Edition: March 2014.
Photographs by Shutterstock.

ISBN-13: 978-1494265588

ISBN-10: 1494265583

9
STEPS
TO INFLUENCE

A MENTALIST'S GUIDE FOR EVERYMAN

By Ehud Segev

Published by

MENTALIZER EDUCATION

To Nimrod.

TABLE OF CONTENTS

ABOUT THE AUTHOR	9
THE HIDDEN KNOWLEDGE	14
STEP 1: SMILE!	23
STEP 2: LISTEN	34
STEP 3: FOCUS	52
STEP 4: UNDERSTAND	82
STEP 5: MEMORIZE	99
STEP 6: RELAX	114
STEP 7: ATTITUDE	132
STEP 8: BE HAPPY	146
STEP 9: CONFIDENCE	158
FINAL WORDS	179

ABOUT THE AUTHOR

World renowned mentalist **Ehud Segev**, aka The Mentalizer, was born in 1979 in the Israeli city of Safed, long known as the spiritual center of the Jewish world. In the 16th century, Safed emerged as the City of Kabbalah. Most of the great scholars and Rabbis who studied and taught the secrets of Kabbalah, an esoteric school of thought native to Judaism, lived in this great city and it is also where Ehud Segev began his spiritual destiny.

Growing up in the Upper Galilee in the 1980's, Ehud chose to spend his time unlike other boys his age. While neighborhood children were outside playing, 12 year old Segev was inside reading books on mind reading, non-verbal communication, and mysticism. Though the town's librarian was alarmed to see such a young boy delve into such cryptic studies, Ehud's mother was not; she had always known there was something different about her son.

"When I was twelve, I took the entire shelf of books that dealt with mysticism and spiritualism from the library and my mother had to sign a permission form, since I was considered too young for those topics. The librarian may have thought I had lost my mind but my mother was ever so supportive. I'll never forget that," says Segev.

His reputation for having a connection to the universe and his capability to read minds, analyze behavior and influence people, set the stage for his worldwide success.

At the age of 16, he was featured on the Israeli news for his unique ability; one that some people consider magic and others consider spirituality. Segev has another way of explaining it; he refers to his "powers" as "magic from the mind."

"Others call it intuition. I don't. I call it the knowledge to connect. The more YOU KNOW, the more you're able to connect to yourself and then to others. The more you are connected, the bigger the miracles you can perform in your life. I don't have any supernatural powers -on the contrary- my powers are so natural that they are super natural.

In my shows and lectures throughout the world, I combine my special abilities as a performer with magic and spirituality. My goal: to make this world a better place and to help people realize that our deepest desires aren't materialistic, but spiritual. If I can use all the publicity, stage-presence and my TV appearances to bring people closer to the light, my destiny is fulfilled," added Segev.

Fascination with the "super natural" boy continued and at the age of 19, he continued to shock and amaze throughout Israel. In one newspaper article titled "The Prophecy", Segev predicted who would win the race for the mayors' chair, in several cities.

The article was published 11 days before the elections took place. With only a photo to reference, Segev, as he put it, "used his mentalism abilities to mentally analyze each candidate and foresee the winners."

Segev was 100% right. This is when people started calling him the Mental Analyzer; soon after to be nicknamed -The Mentalizer.

A few years later, Segev became one of a small percentage of entertainers that signed an exclusive contract with the US army to entertain far away troops in bases around the world. For this he received a coin of excellence -a special award for extraordinary contribution - which was the basis for obtaining an EB-1 classification from the U.S. Department of Homeland Security and lead to him becoming a permanent resident in America.

According to United States Citizenship and Immigration Services requirements, in order to qualify for the prestigious EB-1 classification, you must have an extraordinary ability and be "one of that small percentage who have risen to the very top of the field of endeavour."

Now performing in different forums all around the world, including being featured on shows such as NBC's series "Phenomenon" as well as on numerous Israeli television networks and radio stations, Segev's reputation is an overwhelmingly positive one.

He combines his talents as a performer with magic, spirituality, his unique connection to people and deep understanding of human psychology and behavior, to provide mind blowing performances and enlightening entertainment.

But Ehud is concerned with providing people with something much more than just entertainment; he strives to convey a message of connection to one's inner sense, and hopes that by watching him, his audience gains a deeper understanding of the wonders and mysteries of the universe, and life.

He also seeks to help people understand how they can put to practice some of his techniques to use in their own lives, through his program "How to Be a Mental Analyzer". Based on in-depth studies of human behavior patterns and the psyche, Segev believes anyone can learn his techniques of Neuro-linguistic programming and interpreting non-verbal communication, in order to enhance all their daily interactions. His belief is that these abilities can be used by anyone, to further good in the world and better humanity one person at a time.

"Yes, I am gifted. And I am now here to share this phenomenal gift with you. Each one of us is a prophet and each one of us is a leader in his own way. It's just about using these tools to discover the magic and potential within ourselves. Everyone can learn to take advantage of these tools. Eveyone is born gifted; they just haven't been shown the path to discovering their inner gold. I'm going to give you the methods to start uncovering the treasure that is you."

THE HIDDEN KNOWLEDGE

> **People are more what they hide than what they show.**

THE HIDDEN KNOWLEDGE

Have you ever wanted to be considered extraordinary? Have you ever wanted to have the sense of self which made you comfortable with everything and everyone around you?

What would you do if you had the power to READ people and know what they were thinking and feeling? Imagine what you could do if every detail, every word, every gesture, every subtle hint that was ever presented before you, would be noticed by your keen all-seeing senses!

If you could use this information in order to influence others and succeed in every arena of your life, would you take a few hours from your day to discover your previously untapped potential?

If you'd like to learn the hidden knowledge from those mind manipulators, body language connoisseurs, non-verbal communication experts, human psychology and behavior specialists known as Mentalists, then this is the book for you!

Like Patrick Jane from the successful TV show "THE MENTALIST", you will come to understand how these masters of the mind harness their powers, not only to READ people and situations, but to INFLUENCE them as well.

The power of Mentalism will offer you a mental advantage that far surpasses that of your peers. It will give you the confidence to expand your possibilities, and see a whole new world; a world within the one that you've been living in all along, but never even noticed!

In fact, with these revealed discoveries, I will venture to say that you will be able to do just about anything!

Does all that sound good? Are you thinking the learning process will be too long, that you don't have the ability, time, or resources? Now, what if I were to tell you that there are just 9 simple "keys" to becoming a great mentalist AND all of them are straightforward and easy to accomplish?

I call them my secret "magic" nine steps because of the astounding results you will achieve if you practice them every day; although there is absolutely no "hocus pocus" or "abracadabra" involved.

The potential to learn these key steps lies within every one of us. Sometimes it is "out there" for everyone to see; other times it is buried deep within us, yearning to be set free. Whether lying just beneath the surface, or entrenched within the subconscious, these capabilities are all a part of our human disposition.

With the right tools and some digging, these abilities will be unearthed, allowing you to do things that may now seem impossible.

My full program, "How To Be a Mental Analyzer", is a step-by-step guide to becoming a more focused, more alert, happier, calmer, and more positive individual. This program has transformed thousands world-wide into real life Mentalizers (Mental Analyzers) or as the world likes to call them: Mentalists.

Students have accomplished a vast expansion in their skill sets, developed better decision-making abilities, improved their analytical processes, enhanced their social skills, helped their careers and strengthened their relationships.

How have they achieved such drastic changes in their lives? I can assure you, it is not anything otherworldly and if you are willing to put forth the effort, it is nothing that is out of your reach.

Through the topics explored, students have developed the ability to understand and interpret body language and speech patterns, "read" minds, meditate, practice self-hypnosis and so much more, all by discovering the power of their own mind! Once I provided them with the keys to unlocking those traits within themselves, their possibilities became limitless!

But since this program takes months to master (if not years!), many students became impatient. They wanted some kind of quick reference material to enable them to dive right in and apply their education to real life circumstances and situations.

So they requested a guide, or cheat sheet so to speak, of the essential tools that every mentalist must have, but do not demand years of practice to implement. Therein was the idea behind the creation of this book.

Just so you'll understand: My students pay me $1,970 dollars for my live training, or $499 dollars for the online course! So getting this book for only $14.99 is a true bargain! For the price of what most of us spend on our daily lunch, you'll be able to change your life for good! You have absolutely nothing to lose and so much valuable knowledge to gain!

So there you have it! This concise book is a foretaste of my $2,000 complete program. You will learn the 9 keys of the most basic, practical, straightforward and influential information on how you can develop and expand your mental skills and become a mentalizer. The thousands of students enrolled in my programs have sent me terrific feedback; they exuberantly express what a powerful impact these tools have had on their daily lives and now you will be able to utilize this information too for a fraction of the cost!

Here are just a few things my students have written to me during my course:

Francine De Ocampo · New Era University: "My whole week is not complete without a lesson from Ehud! I learn so much from him. I know I'm in the right path of knowledge. this is really priceless! Thanks for the new wisdom and insight about mentalism!

__Logan F Wade:__ "This is a great structure for learning about the mind and its uncontrollable tendencies and sociological aspects."

Todd A Fonseca · Fellow · Marquette University: "As a hypnosis practitioner, the importance of calibrating is critical to success - I'm certain this will help catapult my success to new levels."

Dianne Ruth · Union Institute & University: "I am a doctor of clinical & counselling psychology, a board certified master of NLP and a board certified master of medical and clinical hypnotherapy. I am excited and looking forward to learning and developing new ways to use and direct my knowledge. Thanks!"

Mehvr Ismael: "I always wanted to enhance my knowledge and seek the full potential of my brain and these lessons are just the thing I wanted!"

Tamara Sager Burkhart · VCU: "I am so excited to have found this program! Thank you so much for making it available!"

Froilan James Miguel · Global City Innovative College: "I wish to be the best that I can be. I know this program can change me and by changing the way I think, speak, move, and look at the world, it'll help me make it a better place. Thanks for this wonderful opportunity."

Roberto Torres · Sarasota High School: "What a great opportunity this is for anyone who wishes to better themselves and understand the world around."

Jason Yap · NAFA | Nanyang Academy Of Fine Arts: "I feel that mentalism is a very practical way to enhance the relationships with the people around me, and I feel it is interesting to read somebody's mind and know what is the reason behind everything they do."

Leonardo Silva · Olinda, Brazil: "Thank you for taking the time to teach this powerful skill to starters like me. I've been waiting for this opportunity for a long time now and can't wait to learn and put these skills into practice to help other people realize how much life has to offer."

Think of the key steps I offer in this guide, as "appetizers" that precede the "main course." If you enjoy these appetizers, then maybe you are ready to take the next steps to becoming a professional mental analyzer.

"What? Something so terrific is simple AND it costs less than 15 bucks? No way!"

If that's what you are thinking, I congratulate you because it means that you are using your brain to analyze the information given to you–and that, my friend, is the foundation upon which the field of mentalism is built.

Are you ready to find out what the hype is all about? Great!

Let's get started!

Writing the first step for a guide like this takes a lot of thought. The first must be the strongest, most valuable of them all and provide the essence of how to influence people.

However, it cannot be too difficult or complicated, lest you create the fear that the road to becoming a mentalist is far too arduous-which is NOT the case.

It will take hard work, but I assure you that everyone has the mental stamina to use this knowledge in order to function like a mentalist and influence people, given your heart is truly in your quest.

So, what is this one thing that separates a mentalist from the rest? What gives the mentalist the ability to tap into other people's thoughts and emotions in order to influence the way they think or behave?

First, the mentalist must be 'welcomed' into their world in order to achieve these great feats.

What is the most potent and yet most simple thing an individual can do to gain access into another's personal mental zone?

The answer is:

❝ When you're smilin' the whole world smiles with you!

STEP 1: SMILE!

The lyrics from the famous song from last century still hold important, relevant and usable knowledge for today - Smile and the world smiles back! Yes, it's true, even in those notoriously "cold hearted" places like New York City!

Why? Because smiling is an "emotional contagion." What? Smiling is contagious? Yes! Yes it is. And if you can have someone mimic your expressions, then wham! you've just brought them into your zone of influence.

How does this work?

The phrase "emotional contagion" embodies the idea that people will synchronize their personal feelings with those around them - whether consciously or unconsciously; and thus, a sensibility conveyed by one person will become "contagious" to others. They are then tied together emotionally-they reflect each other's emotional states. Psychologist Elaine Hatfield, theorized that this is best evidenced by the mirror reflection or mimicry of people's expressions, postures, movements and vocalizations. So, if someone is happy and smiles, the smile will be reflected back by the people surrounding them. They are now on an equal emotional footing, in a similar state of mind, and share the same behavioral attitudes; and therefore, are best set to exchange information on a deeper interpersonal level.

Even Edgar Allan Poe utilized this concept in his story "The Purloined Letter." In a precursor to modern day detective stories, the Protagonist, in an effort to read the mind of a subject of interest, mimics the facial expressions of that person to see which emotions are invoked within him.

There are several distinct theories as to why a physical act can trigger an emotional response. One is the classical conditioning approach, where people automatically associate a smile with feeling happy. For example, Pavlov's dogs were conditioned to associate the sound of a bell with the obtainment of food; so the bell sound itself then triggered the physical yearning of hunger within the dogs. Much like these canine subjects, we too can be conditioned by outside stimuli. We see a smile and expect the person wearing it to be happy. Once the connection is made, smiling in and of itself is enough to generate a physical feeling of happiness. Another theory is that the actual gestures of the smile, the physical movements that comprise it, trigger a chemical reaction in the brain that stimulates the production of "happy hormones".

Which ever theory may dominate, one thing still holds true: smiling is a behavior which can be found to mean the same thing - 'I am happy', in every society on earth. As the American writer Max Eastman so eloquently put it: "A smile is the universal welcome."

No matter what country or culture, or even species! a genuine, bright smile will never be lost in translation! Every society on Earth recognizes a smile and assigns similar qualities to them as well as "smile" through body language! And, it has been scientifically shown that animals can read a smiling face and attribute approachability to that person.

This is by no means true for other behaviors and gestures - some of which mean wildly different things when removed from one culture and performed in another.

Why does smiling have such amazing effects?

With this universal acceptance and appeal a smile becomes a most powerful weapon. It can warm another's soul, indicate acceptance or appreciation, portray happiness and contentment, and signify that you are open to another's presence or ideas. It can disarm a person who is confrontational, or brighten a person's day when they are glum. How powerful that "simple" grin can be!

When I was younger going through some turbulent times as we all do, I received a plaque as a gift which contains these wise words:

> **Smile, it makes people wonder what you've been up to."**

Think about that statement for a moment.

Anything you can do which causes another to pause and become interested in you, creates an atmosphere in which they can be drawn into a zone where you can have influence over them. Because, then, they have entered into YOUR world, instead of merely passing you by. And no one has greater control over your world, then you.

I've even used this smiling technique in tense business negotiations. In the middle of serious discussions, I might suddenly smile. It breaks up the moment; causes the other people involved to pause, step away from their train of thought. It disarms them. And once this happens, the control bounces back into your court, so to speak. You have an advantage.

Next time you're in a heated discussion, with anyone, break into a smile and see how the situation takes a sharp turn from the negative.

Remember, not a smug know-it-all smile, but a genuine, full teeth showing smile. You'll be amazed at the transformation in the environment.

Smiling is also a terrific "people magnet". Wouldn't you rather be in the company of a smiling person than a glum one? Of course you would! That's just human nature.

People will usually avoid a person who doesn't project a friendly and welcoming personality. Would YOU want to have a relationship with a person who is always morose-looking? He or she sends out a non-verbal message that shouts: "STAY AWAY FROM ME!"

Unlike a gloomy person, a smiling one conveys a completely different, more upbeat message: "C'mon over and open yourself up to me, because I am a friendly and likable kind of guy (or gal)!"

Yes, a great smile is one of the most important keys to a successful life – both professional and personal. There's a wonderful example of this thought. Many years ago at Christmas time, a large New York City Department store noticed the low morale of many of its sales clerks. The crowds and pressures of selling in that season were taking its toll on their staff. They also noticed their customers were suffering from similar Holiday blues. So they published an advertisement that offered this simple but sage philosophy. It read as follows:

The Value Of A Smile At Christmas

It costs nothing, but creates much. It enriches those who receive, without impoverishing those who give. It happens in a flash and the memory of it sometimes lasts forever, None are so rich they can get along without it, and none so poor but are richer for its benefits.

It creates happiness in the home, fosters good will in a business, and is the countersign of friends. It is rest to the weary, daylight to the discouraged, sunshine to the sad, and Nature's best antidote fee trouble.

Yet it cannot be bought, begged, borrowed, or stolen, for it is something that is no earthly good to anybody till it is given away. And if in the last-minute rush of Christmas buying some of our Sales people should be too tired to give you a smile, may we ask you to leave one of yours? For nobody needs a smile so much as those who have none left to give!

A simple gesture, such a potent impact. This fact is even borne out by scientific research: A 2007 study published in the Journal of the Human Evolution and Behavior showed that a smiling person sends out a signal that people can trust and cooperate with him.

So if you want your colleagues, friends, loved ones, employers, employees, customers, ANYONE to be responsive to your desires, cultivate a killer smile! Not only is smiling a valued asset for interpersonal transactions, but did you know that a smile can also benefit your own health? How is that, you wonder? Just listen to what experts tell us:

The act of smiling actually stimulates centers in the brain which signal pleasure neurotransmitters and the production of "happy" hormones such as Endorphins, Oxytocin and Serotonin - which change your mood for the better.

British researchers have discovered that one smile can generate the same level of "happy" chemical reactions within the brain as 2,000 bars of chocolate! Furthermore, a smile is similar in terms of brain reward as receiving £16,000 ($25,000) in cash!

Smiling relieves stress and anxiety:

The mere act of turning up your lips reduces the level of stress inducing hormones such as cortisol and adrenaline, thereby lowering your blood pressure and boosting your immune system.

It is well documented that a person who projects health and vitality is more likely to possess positions of leadership and authority. Leaders and authority figures are more likely to have the ability to control the path of the thoughts and actions of those around them; so once again, a simple smile can enhance your mesmerizing mentalism mechanisms!

Furthermore, this effect has social ramifications. A smiling person is perceived as more competent, courteous, happier, easier to get along with, and physically more attractive.

As I mentioned in the introductory chapter, the powerful mentalism techniques that I am outlining in this guide are easily put into practice. Smiling is, hands down, the simplest and most "achievable" of them all!

Now, only a sincere smile, which radiates from your heart, will do. And, by the way, it's not just your lips that are set in a smile; the best most genuine ones also come from your eyes.

In fact, many facial muscles must work together in harmony to produce a "winning" smile. Know this: a sincere smile should come from "a happy place" within you. It's not something you can just "manufacture" at will. You really have to work on your mindset and emotions first, so that your smile reflects your true inner self.

Try it now! Close your eyes and think of a happy memory. Take a deep breath and immerse yourself in that memory!

Feel its revitalizing juices overtake you and your muscles start to relax. You should feel your whole body react to this memory and soon, a genuine smile will cross your face. Now, open your eyes. Your mood and your disposition, if this exercise was done correctly, should have improved and you should be feeling more energized. While allowing yourself the pleasure of enjoying this smile, your mind should be clearer and your eyes should be sparkling. You will feel it within yourself and once you do, know that others will notice it too!

- There is no better way to have a genuinely appealing smile than to:
- Show appreciation for people's thoughts and enjoy their company.
- Be interested and engaged when in conversation.
- Be a positive, optimistic, and emotionally balanced person.

Are you wondering how you can become such a person, especially if you have a mostly negative and pessimistic mindset? There IS a way of altering your feelings and developing your happy side, through proven techniques such as Neuro Linguistic Programming (NLP), self-hypnosis, and meditation.

Just as a quick example: With an NLP technique called "anchoring," you can be in control of your emotions, turning a negative habit, behavior or mindset, into a positive one. And with "Mindful" meditation, you can find inner peace and emotional balance within yourself. I will go into NLP and Mindful meditation in a bit more depth, later on.

For now, I would like for you to try a pleasant exercise. Tomorrow when you wake up, put on a genuine smile and make it a point to show your smile to the world! See how they react. Your show of happiness should not be boisterous or obnoxious. Just, while you are walking down the hall or in the grocery store, or in the office or wherever the day may take you, look people in the eye and smile at them.

If you would like to up the ante a little bit, try to find opportunities to help people out during the day, smiling all the while! Hold doors open for people, pick up dropped items, get things that may be out of their reach - simple, yet potent gestures all enhanced by a flash or your pearly whites. Chances are, most of them will smile back, say hi, or maybe even initiate conversation with you. People are drawn to happiness. Who knows, just by being genuinely happy and friendly to people, you might have made a huge impact on their day!

So smiling really is a super power which enables you to communicate how well your life is going to other people around you (even perhaps when things could be better).

In the appropriate situations, there is no such thing as too much smiling. So increase the amount that you smile and notice the benefits that it may bring; not just to your social life but also to your health and wellbeing. Try the following exercises below if you feel that your smiling "technique" could use some work:

The Pencil in the Mouth

Feeling a bit down? Want to feel happier? Try this. Take a pencil and place it in your mouth so that it pushes against its sides forcing you to smile.

This phenomenon is called biological feedback and fools your brain into thinking you are happy simply because you are smiling.

If you want to experiment with this effect, try putting the pencil on your moustache line and holding it there. You will notice that you begin to frown and feel a bit unhappy.

Don't worry though; a quick look into the nearest mirror will alleviate the effect by making you laugh at your face, causing the pencil to drop.

Smile at people

The next time you are in a public place smile at someone. A member of the opposite sex is usually best or someone who is working (bus driver, receptionist).

Notice how they respond. I am willing to bet that most of the time (if not, all of the time) people will smile back (provided your smile is genuine and not faked!).

Practice your real smile in the mirror before doing this by thinking of genuinely happy feelings and notice the sensations. Then repeat this whenever you require a golden smile.

Stop for a second and ask yourself if you truly, completely, understand why SMILING is the first lesson in the mentalist influence guide; only after you acknowledge this basic understanding, move on to the new chapter.

Remember that a mentalist is a people decoder. He reads them. He understands them. He 'feels' them and knows what they are feeling too. If you can't create the right type of 'bonding' with the people around you - you will never succeed in becoming a real mentalist and therefore will never be able to influence any one.

So now you have your mentalism step number one: be "Contagious!" Just crack a smile, and see how people respond to you!

Which brings us right into step number two.

> **The most basic of all human needs is the need to understand and be understood. The best way to understand people is to listen to them.**

- Ralph G. Nichols

STEP 2: LISTEN

Put on your listening ears! In one episode of the TV show "The Mentalist," Patrick Jane (played by Simon Baker), is asked by someone who is amazed by his abilities: "Are you a psychic?" Patrick replies: "No, but I know how to listen!"

And that, dear friend, is one of the most important "tools" a mentalizer – and ALL people - should possess. Unfortunately, this is often not the case.

The second key then is to listen. This is one of the most important secrets of being a mentalist. Later you will see how listening compounds the other abilities you will soon develop, but for now let's concentrate and comprehend how listening will bring you much closer to your goal of analyzing people and influencing them.

First, let's look at the short list of reasons most people should or do listen:

- To extract information from a situation.
- To understand people or concepts.
- To learn.
- For mere enjoyment.

Well, these are the reasons that if asked, people would say they listen but in practice, it's not what they are truly doing at all. Have you noticed when you interact with another person or with a group, that a lot of people talk about themselves continually, but only rarely (if ever) show interest in anyone else? They're not really learning anything; they're not truly understanding what is being said; they're not really focused enough to enjoy the content.They're just there in body, but their mind is really not into the conversation. Are you one of these people? Maybe to you "listening" means nodding your head and pretending to hear what someone tells you, while your mind bounces all over the place like a Mexican Jumping Bean on a trampoline? That's NOT listening! Ask yourself this question: how much of what you hear do you actually remember? Chances are you only retain a small part of what people tell you.

In fact, studies suggest that we remember only between 25 percent and 50 percent of what we hear. In other words, we forget between half and three-quarters of the things people convey to us – as the saying goes, "in one ear and out the other." That is certainly not conducive to excelling at studies, work, or social relationships.

The thing that distracts most people, even aspiring mentalists, is that while other people are speaking you will listen to what they have to say in order to try to answer or give your own opinion. So, really, you are not "listening" to them. The biggest problem is we do not listen to understand, we listen to reply.

Like a lioness hunting prey, you are listening, waiting in the bushes for your chance to pounce; you are listening for that moment of weakness in the conversation where you can jump in and monopolize the conversation with your own statement.

Listening, really listening, is paying attention, showing genuine interest, openness and curiosity in what other people tell you.

Two types of listening exist. The first is Passive listening. This is what the majority of people do most of the time. They get the gist of what is being said but then they fail to get the real details of what was being conveyed.

This is the equivalent of reading every other line in this book. You will get an impression of what I am trying to say but you will not get the full impact of these techniques.

The type of listening that every mentalist needs to develop is called Active Listening. This is where your entire focus and full concentration is on the speaker. Your mind is silent and you are just absorbing everything that the speaker says without conscious refutations or preparing your next line. Conversations like these contain a lot of silence because this is when all the thinking takes place. While each person is speaking, the other individual is fully concentrating on ensuring that they are hearing and interpreting the other person's ideas and content correctly.

> **Most of the successful people I've known are the ones who do more listening than talking.**
> –*Bernard M. Baruch (Wall Street Wizard, financier, political consultant, statesman)*

If you are an attentive listener, you will not only learn new things and pick up subtle hints, but you will also come across as a caring and trustworthy human being.

If people imbue their trust in you, they will reveal more about themselves. And knowledge is power! The more you know about a person, their thought processes and their beliefs, the better you will be able to find the correct path into their minds which, in turn, will then allow you to instil your desires into their thoughts.

Once they have internalized your desires, voilà, you have gained influence over their behaviors and actions.

However, let me make it perfectly clear: I am not suggesting that you should PRETEND to listen and be interested just to make people trust you and confide in you. That would be totally unacceptable! (Besides, people can usually spot a fake pretty quickly, even without any mentalist training at all!) No, I am saying that all these qualities should be GENUINE and come from the heart.

It is all about feeling. Just as you know when you are being lied to, or even if there is something not quite right about a person, situation or conversation, others will know if you are really listening to them, or putting on a facade.

When one person is genuinely listening to another, there is a bond that is mutually shared and felt simultaneously.

What if you are not a natural-born listener? Don't worry, you can learn and develop this skill! I talk about this in more detail in my full program, "How to be a Mental Analyzer," where I share some very effective tips on how to become a better, more attuned listener. These techniques are really easy to learn, but you would be surprised, maybe even shocked, at how many people don't even try to master them.

Again, it is all about effort. A lot of these steps are simple, in theory; however, few people are willing to take the time for self improvement.

I can only provide the route to becoming a mentalist and the keys that will help you influence others, but you must unlock the door yourself. Let me share with you the most important thing that I teach my students; the main key to being a good listener, is "conscious" listening. For instance:

Focus not only on words, but, more importantly, on the entire message the person conveys to you. Don't interrupt or jump in mid-sentence – you are not listening in order to reply, but in order to learn; your intent is to fully understand the person in front of you. The difference in actively listening is not to respond, but instead, listen in order to study their personality. What bothers them? Why are they feeling that way? What has led up to them feeling that way?

Once the person stops talking, certainly show your interest by asking open-ended questions that are relevant to what they just told you. However, formulate the question in a non-judgmental way, inviting a response that gives you further insight into the person's thoughts and feelings.

Additionally, it is okay to think about these questions for a moment after they stop speaking. Silence is okay. Although it may put the other person on edge at first, once they understand that you were genuinely absorbing all of the information they just entrusted you with, and are pausing in order to respond in the most effective, appropriate way, they will appreciate the time you are taking to help them with whatever is bothering them.

One of the techniques used in counselling and psychotherapy is that of Active Listening. This is where one encourages a person to talk about themselves, they listen attentively to what the person has said, and then it is repeated back to them in a paraphrased manner.

The man considered the Father of Psychoanalysis, Sigmund Freud, was renowned for many things, but mostly for his ability to make others feel that he was TRULY interested in what they were revealing to him. One of his acquaintances said the following about the manner in which he listened:

"It struck me so forcibly that I shall never forget him. He had qualities which I had never seen in any other man. Never had I seen such concentrated attention. There was none of that piercing 'soul penetrating gaze' business. His eyes were mild and genial. His voice was low and kind. His gestures were few. But the attention he gave me, his appreciation of what I said, even when I said it badly, was extraordinary. You've no idea what it meant to be listened to like that."

Few of us will ever possess the overall talents of Sigmund Freud. But his is a model to emulate. And you can start with the Active Listening techniques. The paraphrasing of the communication, acts as a method of clarification between you and the speaker, and ensures that they know that you have made a correct interpretation of their message. For example, using A.L. the following idea might be communicated:

I am concerned that I am not going to be able to complete this work on time. It's all getting too much to handle and I am worried that I may have to abort the project. I don't want to do this because then I will have felt like I have failed.

[Pause for consideration by the listener]

You feel that you would be a failure if you don't complete the project and that it is becoming a bit too much for you to cope with. You are worried you may not be able to complete the work on time. What does it mean if the work is not completed on time?

You can see that all of the central themes of the statement have been reflected back to the speaker by the listener but not necessarily using the same language!

The idea here is to change the order or the flow of the content and to adjust some words; otherwise, the participant could become a little bit uncomfortable that they are being parroted, and perhaps mocked. This process will also make it easier for you to remember what has been said (as you are using your own language). It will also help to clarify certain points with the speaker who may refute some of your vocabulary; thus enabling you to get an even better idea of how they feel.

This process will establish or build rapport with the person with whom you are communicating; it will facilitate further communication and ensure that they regard you as a good and attentive listener.

The crucial point here is the addition of an open question at the end of the listener's summation of what has been said. This entire procedure enables both the listener and the speaker to know that they are both 'on the same page'; the listener further demonstrates his attentiveness by asking subsequent relevant questions, to the speaker, in order to gather information.

It is a process of validation between the speaker and the listener and helps to ensure that the correct message is always communicated between both parties.

You can practice your Active listening skills with anyone. The next time you are having a conversation, try Active listening and see what reaction you get. If the person knows you well they may notice that something has changed but they will probably not be able to put their finger on precisely what you are doing. They will certainly feel like they are being listened to and appreciated and therefore, probably won't offer much resistance.

Use this technique wisely, for if you start using it all the time it may lose its power. Repeating back everything that your pizza delivery driver says on the phone is not likely to achieve anything other than a more expensive phone bill. But try it, and see what happens. You might get more than you bargained for!

The most important thing to remember when engaging in conversation, from which to extract information, is that you have to speak about things that hold interest to the other person.

Publilius Syrus, an old Roman poet, summed this up nicely and succinctly, when he remarked - "We are interested in others when they are interested in us."

The best way to show interest in a person is to first and foremost, make sure you interject their name, if you know it, into the conversation; if you don't know it, make sure you inquire as to what it is. But make sure you remember the name exactly. If it's one which you can't recall easily, ask them to spell it. If you don't repeat the name correctly, the other person will be insulted and most likely close down and not be receptive to what you're saying. Many politicians are coached on this very subject. They are told: "To recall a voter's name is statesmanship. To forget it is oblivion."

This topic is so important, I'm going to take a moment and cite a passage from Motivational speaker and writer Dale Carnagie:

> **We should be aware of the magic contained in a name and realize that this single item is wholly and completely owned by the person with whom we are dealing and nobody else. The name sets the individual apart; it makes him or her unique among all others. The information we are imparting or the request we are making takes on a special importance when we approach the situation with**

the name of the individual. From the waitress to the senior executive, the name will work magic as we deal with others."

Every great leader in the world, knows that the way to engage a person, and ultimately turn them around on their beliefs, is first to show genuine interest in what the other treasures most.

For many, that topic is Me, Myself, and I; "Talk to people about themselves, and they will listen for hours" - this quote by Benjamin Disreaeli, the brilliant debater, novelist and English Prime Minister, fully encompasses the thought.

So, first engage someone by the use their name, then go to compliments concerning things you may see or be aware of - turn to their family, or accomplishments.LISTEN ATTENTIVELY to how they respond then turn your attention to how what you have learned may serve to benefit you. This is imperative in any interaction you may have.

These techniques are incredibly beneficial, not only with friends or strangers but when having discussions with people who are significant in your life. You may have a desire, you may have a need you wish to be satisfied, but instead of forging ahead with your own "I want", "I need diatribe", first make the person you wish to influence, the center of your focus. Jack Woodford wrote in Strangers in Love:

"Few human beings, are proof against the implied flattery of rapt attention." I went even further than giving him rapt attention. I was "hearty in my approbation and lavish in my praise."

You've lavished your attention, and you've used your Active listening skills, rephrasing what the other person is relating in the conversation.

I will guarantee that you have now embarked into a situation where your needs will ultimately be met; because, you now have the knowledge of the other person's needs and desires, so you can utilize this to formulate the presentation of your wants; you can use the information gathered from your prior interactions to tailor the situation to your benefit, by showing the other person that the desired path is beneficial to them also.

You are now in the best position to offer them something they might want, (because you've listened to what it is!) in return for giving you want you wish. This is called the Rule of Reciprocation; it is one of the most potent compliance techniques around. Reciprocal concessions are found to be an underlying factor in human social interactions. Anthropologist, Richard Leakey believes the rule of reciprocity is

"a defining element of what it means to be human. We are human because our ancestors learned to share their food and their skills in an honoured network of obligation."

Cultural anthropologists Tiger and Fox, coined the term "web of indebtedness" to describe this phenomenon.

They believed that: "It is the foundation for such diverse human practices as the division of labour, exchange of goods and services, evolution of experts, and other interdependencies that connect humans into more efficient cooperative units.

As a result, we are trained at an early age to comply with the rule of reciprocity."

So remember, to get something that you want, it is best to offer something that is wanted. Mutual satisfaction is key. You can not obtain mutual satisfaction, if you are not listening to the other person who is part and parcel to you obtaining your desires.

In a relationship, learning what makes your significant other tick - what makes them scared, knowing their deepest wishes and dreams, will enable you to have a positive influential effect on them and the relationship as a whole.

You must appeal to those characteristics of the person you love. And to repeat, if you understand how a person approaches and reacts to situations, you can utilize this knowledge to foster behavior from them that will facilitate the most satisfactory resolution of a situation, for you. And while doing so, make them happy that they were able to make you happy. Win, win.

If you should encounter resistance, don't despair.

Don't try to force your will onto another. They will not change their mind, and will only double down on their opposition to you.

As Benjamin Franklin said:

> **A man convinced against his will.
> Is of the same opinion still.**

Instead, identify precisely your needs and objectives; offer valid and logical reasons behind your wants that appeal to the sensibilities of the person you are trying to inspire to act in a way that pleases you.

Studies conducted by Havard Psychologist and Professor, Ellen Langer, demonstrated that people are most likely to comply with a request if any reason is given, even if the reason really makes no sense; it seems the mere request activates an automatic compliance response-one that was instilled in us as children. We are taught as youngsters to react positively to people who ask something of us when they back up their request, with a reason.

In Langer's study where students were lined up to use a school photocopier, the following fascinating occurrences were documented: "When students further back in line asked, "Excuse me, I have five pages, may I use the Xerox?" 60 percent agreed to the request; 40 percent, however, said no and continued with their own copying. When a reason was added — "Excuse me, I have five pages, may I use the photocopier, I'm in a rush" — 94 percent agreed to the request. However, what doesn't make sense is why the same number agreed when the request was changed to "Excuse me, may I use the Xerox because I want to make copies." This reasoning is just plain ridiculous.

Why would you use a photocopier if you were not planning to make copies? It is the same as no reason at all. Langer's conclusion: Most of the people did not think about the request at all. They mindlessly complied."

So always remember, if you have opposition, back up your request with at least some kind of supposition.

Since influential people are often the best teachers, this skill is one that is applicable to every situation where information is in need of being conveyed and a desired goal obtained.

Influencing people is a talent everyone should possess. Especially when it is being used for good purposes like helping others make the right decision in life.

An example of this is in the class room where a good teacher will listen to his students and really study who they are and how they think in order to find the right teaching strategy for them.

These are just the basic steps you need to know. Of course, there is much more to learn if you decide that you're fascinated by this field.

In my full program I expand on this theme quite a bit, adding other pertinent information, such as body language communication and other non-verbal behavior techniques: for example, you must listen to the subtle messages conveyed by someone's vocal pitch, pace, tone, volume and rhythm in order to receive the person's entire message.

By doing these things correctly, you will almost be able to actually read the minds of the people talking to you! But this information can fill up an entire new book!

Here is another exercise for you: Strike up a conversation with someone and try your best to listen as you would normally do. Then write down in detail how much you remember from what that person said.

Next, strike up a conversation with either the same or another person, and try to actively listen, practicing the lesson that I just talked about. Then, write down what you remember of the conversation. Chances are, you will have heard and retained a lot more of what that person said.

Coupled with these skill sets, you will however need to enhance your memory. Worry not, there is also a whole chapter dedicated to improving your memory in this guide so you will soon learn how to retain everything you hear and learn!

This is one of the greatest lessons I can teach you about the secrets of the mentalist. Indeed, you will need to practice the techniques again and again until you master them, but don't worry, you will have plenty of people to practice on!

Everyone is looking for a partner they can talk to. You can be there for them every time. And the best part is that all of this can be achieved through the simple act of opening your ears, absorbing the information you have heard, and reacting in a manner that utilizes the information.

That doesn't sound too difficult now does it? Of course not! It just requires that you pay attention to people you encounter - a must have skill for any successful influential person in any forum.

If you listen carefully to what people tell you, you will not only get to know another person "inside out," but also discover many concepts and ideas that are new to you. You will understand how other people "tick," and how to relate to them, influence them, inspire them and persuade them; all in a positive way, of course.

As you leave this chapter, remember this:

" There's none so blind as those who will not listen.
– *Neil Gaiman*

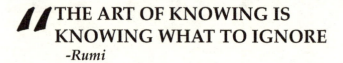
"THE ART OF KNOWING IS KNOWING WHAT TO IGNORE
-Rumi

STEP 3: FOCUS

F-follow

O-one

C-course

U-until

S-successful

The most famous of fictional detectives, Sherlock Holmes, said: "You see, but do not observe. The distinction is clear." Yes, the power of observation! Focusing with an eagle's eye and paying attention to even the most minute and mundane of details is extremely important!

In fact, the ability to observe well, fully absorb what you see, sift through the piles of information and extract all the grains of sand that are the most imperative, is an essential quality for most people, not just detectives.

Because focusing is such a critical skill, I strive to teach my students the best methods to develop a sharpened focus, as well as an acutely alert and attentive mind. There are several simple techniques to achieve these goals and I have included a brief overview of them right here in this quick guide!

But before we talk about HOW to focus, let's first address why people have trouble focusing in the first place. I'm going to introduce you to my thoughts on what has come to be erroneously known as a panacea for humanity but in reality is a detrimental global pandemic- it's what I call Multitasking Influenza.

Enabled by exponential technological advancements, the ability to cram 48 hours of tasks into a 24 hour day seems like the answer to many prayers. It is wonderful in theory, but as in many things, devalued in practice.

Yes, contrary to popular belief, multitasking is NOT your friend. Although an average human being only uses a portion of their brain's capabilities, that function must still be allotted. If you assign all of your brainpower toward one task, the final product can be extraordinary.

If, however, you dispense your allotted brainpower to multiple tasks at one time, you will have many mediocre outcomes and superficial experiences versus what would have been achieved if the task enjoyed singular focus. Unfortunately, it has become the acceptable norm that the quantity of what one can accomplish in an hour is more valuable than the quality of every individual task performed.

Robert Cialdin, a social psychologist, has termed this type of half focused response to stimuli "fixed action patterns" which are brought on by "trigger features". In other words, we have become so immune and overwhelmed with the requirements of a fast paced, technologically inundated society, that we have developed automatic responses to many occurrences. Those events that are similar in nature are grouped together in the mind, and often invoke in us the same response.

The ultimate outcome is that the uniqueness of experiences has been quashed for convenience sake, and to prevent the mind from being overloaded by the copious amounts of responsibilities life in the modern age has brought.

Maybe these results are adequate for most, but it is not the acceptable norm for Mentalists. So how do we rise above the masses and make the most out of our projects, both necessary and enjoyable? We learn how to focus the active parts of our brains, and how to enliven the parts that have lain dormant.

Everything that surrounds you has potential to teach you something. If you are not directly focusing on one task, you will miss key learning elements available to you while you are completing that task. But sometimes it is necessary to do multiple things at once. If this is the case, keep this in mind - it is actually harder to do two similar tasks at the same time, than two very different ones. When performing similar tasks, the mind melds the two, eliminates the distinction, so we lose the individual and idiosyncratic qualities of each - the "fixed action patterns" Robert Cialdin addresses.

So if you have to multitask, make sure you are conducting activities that are different enough that your mind preserves the integrity of each.

American essayist, lecturer and poet Ralph Waldo Emerson said, "Life is a journey, not a destination," and that is exactly what an aspiring mentalist needs to remember. Every breath that you take holds the promise of new life. You need to hold on to that solitary breath, that word, that expression, even if only for a moment, in order to be sure that everything that can be learned from that moment is recognized. As a mentalist, you must train all of your concentration to appreciate and assimilate every inch of your life.

The power of influence starts from within. You cannot be impactful on anyone, or anything, before you have 100% control over your own feelings, thoughts and mind. The same way a mentalist manipulates his external environment to exert influence over it, you must control your internal environment to exercise SELF INFLUENCE; once you obtain, S. I., as I call it, the road is set for you to achieve all of your biggest goals.

Self influence is a derivative of self inspiration. So how do we become self inspired? Studying how to focus will help achieve this mental supremacy.

With practice, this sort of intense concentration will become habit; but at first, you will have to consciously guide and regulate the direction of all of your allotted brainpower to ensure that you are capturing every lesson that each second has to teach. So, with that in mind, here is a little preview of some of the ways you can boost your concentration:

First and foremost, expel Multitasking Influenzia from your body. Give your mind a clean unburdened slate to work with.

This crucial step is more difficult than one may expect; especially in a world where everyone expects multiple maximum performances from one mind at one time.

You must learn how to wisely "spend" your finite amount of mental energy. I use the word "spend", because it consolidates a slightly abstract concept.

This is exactly why you must re-train your brain to focus. You must restrain your allotted mental energy from jumping around all over the place - remember our friend the Mexican Jumping Bean on a trampoline?

Next time you're faced with several "assignments" think about how your brain "bean" is reacting to the thought of accomplishing them all. Begin to prioritize your tasks in a way that allows you to consciously pay your full attention to just one thing at a time; to do this you will first need to set up a list of priorities.

Priority number one:

Give yourself a fighting chance!

"Clear your mind, and the rest will follow."

For now, here's what you should know: extracting and assimilating knowledge about people, places and things within your environment, enables you to proficiently understand the stimuli, of whatever type, that surrounds you; this is how you get to know people in a deep and meaningful way, and not just superficially.

In order to do this, your mind must be clear of any thoughts that might effect what you see.

Some techniques I have found very useful for prepping your mind for acute focus, are relaxation and meditation exercises which utilize calming imagery. In a nut shell, the purpose of meditation is to silence your distractive thoughts, and to elevate your self awareness. Once your mind is a clean slate, you can begin your focal exercises.

I have devoted several lessons in my program to these topics as well as a future book tentatively titled: "The Mentalist's Secret Meditation Guide." Practiced with the right amount of patience and willpower, these modalities can de-clutter your thoughts and prepare your mind for maximum environmental awareness.

Look for this upcoming publication, so you can expand upon these techniques without any lapse in the learning process!

For now, what is most important is to recognize all the environmental triggers that cause your mind "bean" to jump on the trampoline. Determine the things that most often break your concentration and remove them from your vicinity, if possible, for designated periods. That means, get rid of the phones, music, TV, anything that projects loud sounds and blinking lights into your personal space.

It has been determined that the brain can not adequately "metabolize" these types of external stimuli, and still properly digest and internalize the aspects of a situation which must be mindfully responded to and that require maximum mind performance.

Now that you've handled the external distractions, examine honestly your internal distractions. Make a conscious effort to expel from your mind, anything that is causing you to lose concentration on the task at hand-this means, your tests, school, work, relationship problems, anything and everything that gets the bean jumping on the trampoline. Set those things aside; I promise you they'll be there waiting for you once you return from your mindful journey.

The best way to accomplish this, which can be an insurmountable feat for some, is to establish some kind of routine before you set out to perform a task. Do it enough times and it will become a habit. Habits become rituals, and once you have your ritual you can fall into the mindfulness zone much more quickly and easily.

Once you exercise control over your internal and external distractions, you can then prioritize your tasks, direct attention to them consecutively versus simultaneously, and be completely consciously mindful to completing just one thing at a time.

When I was in school, I had a hard time sitting still to study. I'd take out my books, and then start looking around the room and spot a hundred different things in the room that needed attending to. I'd get up, do something, sit down, look up from the book, and see something else. When I finished with that specific room's activities, I'd get up, take my books into the next room, and the whole process would start all over again. Nothing mindful ever got accomplished.

About the only positive thing that came out of my study sessions was that I burned a lot of calories getting up, walking around, sitting down, getting up - that is until I went over to the refrigerator to see what goodies would "help me study"! It was a good thing that even back then I had a really great memory; so, the little time I actually did study, was enough to get me by well enough to accomplish all of my educational goals. Great memories are great! And later on I'll teach you how to make your memories even better! But, see, even now I digress.

When I began to write this book, I had déjà vu all over again. Here were my school days coming back to haunt me. I ended up dividing the writing into two terms. The first - a slow motion one, and the second - a high performance FOCUSED one.

You see, when I first started collecting the material for this book, my mind was still scattered. I would write a few sentences and then check my email. Then I would see if someone sent me an important text message.then that cake on the counter sure looked yummy!

Yes, you see even though I'm an extremely accomplished Mentalist, I'm still human; I'm not perfect.Hard to believe, right??? I kid, but the truth is that once I decided I truly wanted to complete this book, I had to change my mindset completely. The initial process had taken a few months to complete as I wasn't focused.

But once I decided to let go of ALL my internal and external distractions, and I set up my environment in a manner that was most conducive for me to concentrate, well then the magic really started to happen. I developed "tunnel vision." What had taken long tedious months before was completely finished and fine turned in just a few days!

So the best lesson to take out of these anecdotes is you must find out what atmosphere will stimulate your mental magic. Once you do that, what once was deemed unattainable will now not only be conceivable, but undeniably doable. There is that pesky famous cliché, "easier said than done" that I can hear many of you muttering right now.

Yes my story was neat and all, but how exactly do you develop this "tunnel vision"? First, you need to build a tunnel to help focus your vision. What are the foundational blocks to build your tunnel?

Well, we have already spoken about clearing the mind to allow ourselves maximum mental awareness. But, we also must clean out our Mental Filters, which means the belief shields through which we perceive the world. There is a line in the biblical Talmud which reads:

❝ We do not see things as they are, we see things as we are."

What does this mean? There is a term coined by Timothy Leary and made popular by Robert Anton Wilson, which describes the way each person sees the world. It is called a "Reality Tunnel." In essence it means that everyone interprets what they see differently.

Their interpretation of their environment is based upon their experiences, cultures, belief systems, etc. Therefore, according to this theory, everyone's reality is different. However, while realities may be inconsistent, there is only one TRUTH. In this case, truth is defined as an absolute; something that remains constant regardless of time or age or who is making the interpretation regarding, say for instance, an object or fact. For our purposes, mentalizers are seekers of the truth - the constant, absolute, identifiers that comprise a person, place or thing that does not vary depending upon which person is making the observation of same.

Once you are able to obtain the truth about an object, you can act accordingly depending upon your desired goal regarding that object.

But the first thing you will have to be able to do is learn how to see the truth about every object, person, or environment that you see, or you are in. And the way you will be able to do this, is to develop your focus; here is where we come full circle, and have you build another tunnel; however, THIS tunnel, will be the one which will allow you to assimilate truth, vs. idiosyncratic reality. One of the most important lessons you can learn, then, is how to develop, what was previously mentioned, Tunnel VISION.

You are going to engage in a process called Mindfullness. Ellen Langer, Harvard psychologist and professor, originated this term. It involves ridding oneself of the Mental Filters I have just spoken about. It "is the process of actively noticing new things, relinquishing preconceived mindsets, and then acting on the new observations."

With an absolutely clear mind, you are then going to focus on looking at just one thing at a time, rather than allowing your eyes to dart all over the place trying to take in everything at once. Now pick a common object, and write down all the things you have always thought about that item; make a list.

Now, you're going to "re-engage" that object. You're going to focus on it with a newly blank mind, with no pre-conceived notions. Extract every piece of information you can out of this object. Remember, everything has something to teach you. This exercise is training your mind to remember all of the details that comprise this one object; notice the object's color, shape, fragrance – whatever it is about it that makes up its essence. In a less abstract explanation, try to find traits that set it apart from every other object in the world.

Compare and contrast your first list with your second list. This process is a wonderful technique to reprogram your mind and de-clutter your thoughts.

Let me give you a more clear cut example. Imagine there is a soda can next to you. Focus on that soda can and take it all in. What makes that soda can uniquely YOUR soda can? If that can became combined on a table with numerous other soda cans of the same type, how would you know which one was yours to drink? It could be the slight chip on the logo, or the way the lip of the can is bent, but whatever it is, those features make it distinctively yours.

At first, applying this concept to everything you see may sound almost inconceivable; but, as you become better at tunnel vision, you will start a process which I call S.T.V.: Speed Tunnel Vision.

Speed Tunnel Vision will allow you to scan an entire scene (a room, a location, a venue) extremely fast and you will be able to collect the information you need without putting much effort into it.

Do not be mistaken, though, this is not darting all over the place and hoping to catch a glimpse of something useful; this is tunnel vision that runs from one thing to another very fast. By practicing S.T.V. you capture one thing, you retrieve all of the information you can, assimilate everything, and then move on to the next thing in the scene systematically, almost automatically. This procedure only takes a few seconds but it enables you to process the scene in your mind and make important decisions or analysis that may be useful to you later.

Once you have mastered this skill, the difference between you and a typical person entering the same locale, will be vast; you will be enabled to mentally register everything in a location at the speed an average mind would take in a fraction of the surroundings; even if they were paying attention!

Another quality that's very important (and related to the subject of focus) is presence. No, I don't mean being in someone's physical space, what I am referring to is MINDFUL presence. This refers to not only actively listening to and focusing on what someone is telling you, but also observing all the "signals" they are sending out.

Yes, I am talking about non-verbal communication - commonly referred to as body language: posture, facial expressions, gestures, eye movements and other cues that people "communicate" without even knowing it. True, interpreting body language requires skill and practice. But if you faithfully make a diligent effort, you will be able to know someone's thoughts and mindset just by observing their face or posture. (Yes, that is really a skill that you could possess, given the right amount of attentiveness and studiousness.) As I have said before, the human mind is filled with capabilities the average person is never even able to comprehend, let alone utilize.

By taking extra time to scrutinize this specific field, you will be able to realize the full potential your brain possesses, have the ability to challenge it, and to elevate your mental stamina far beyond what you ever thought possible!

The most important rule to observe when dealing with any person in your physical space, from your best friend to a stranger, is to not only listen carefully to what they verbally tell you, but to also keep your eyes wide open and look at them! You are probably thinking: "Of course my eyes are open when I look at someone; how silly."

Well, this is not simply a matter of "looking" at other people, but actually SEEING them and allowing them to see you.

"The Eyes are the window to the soul"; a principle espoused anywhere from the bible, to Sheakespeare to Ralph Waldo Emerson and even by Leonardo Da Vinci.

> **The intellects, the will, are seen in the eye; the emotions, sensibilities, and affections, in the mouth. The animals look for man's intentions right into his eyes. Even a rat, when you hunt him and bring him to bay, looks you in the eye.**
> - *Hiram Powers, American sculptor*

I thought of these quotes immediately for this section, because they illustrate the concept so well.

When interacting with people, it is essential to look at the person you're dealing with actively and intently.

Do not misinterpret, though; I do not mean you should stare awkwardly and make that person uncomfortable. Rather, you should be vigilantly attentive to all of the signs they are unconsciously sending through their motions, gestures and expressions, during your interaction.

This is where focus and concentration come in.

Next time you're sitting with someone, try this: stop and fixate your attention toward things on which you would not normally concentrate. We as human beings are so used to 'mindless talking', that if we were completely honest with ourselves, we would acknowledge that we barely even remember what we spoke about just seconds after we walk away from a conversation.

This is because we have become robotic 'small talkers'; automatically asking questions such as "What's up?" or even "How are you?" without really waiting to hear the answer. You know what I mean. You just naturally expect the person responding will give you an equally robotic answer like "fine, how are YOU"? and thereafter you'd progress to some equally mindless chit chat; each one of you not processing the content of the conversation but only listening for a pause in speaking, so you can eagerly begin to spill your brilliant quips into the "discussion."

By participating in this commonplace useless ritual, the person responding to the initial salutation would feel almost rude if they told you the blatant truth about how they were feeling, even though you had asked.

They might feel sheepish about telling you the truth because then they may feel you were compelled to respond from guilt, with further inquires, and perhaps they really didn't get the vibe from you in the first place that you'd really care to know .and maybe they'd be right.

But how much do you really get to know another person, from this type of empty exchange. Not much right? Certainly not enough to obtain any type of information which you could use in the future.

The point of being consciously aware and processing everything in our environments, is so we can learn from the experience and utilize the information for our benefit.

So, the next time you are entering into a conversation, instead of saying, "Hi, how are you?" and immediately advancing onto the next thought after you hear what you've been previously processing as nothing more than a vocal grunt - STOP, look them in the eye, THEN ask how they are and really listen to their answer.

Even if they reply generically, your genuine interest in their well-being will probably catch them off guard and their body language, their eyes and their tone, will reveal the truth.

If you begin to do this simple gesture, people will begin to take notice. They will automatically appreciate your genuine interest and soon, they may venture from that generic response into something a little more personal. Once you receive that leap of faith, they will begin to trust you and thus, they will be more honest and free with the information they provide you.

Encourage people to talk about themselves. There is nothing more interesting to most people than - me, myself and I. Hone in on what seems to be important to them. Make what is important to them, seem important to you. Monitor your own behavior so as to convey appreciation for what they are telling you. Can you see where this is going?

If you utilize these methods, you'll find out people's strengths and their vulnerabilities. Knowledge is power. Sooner or later you'll have acquired so much beneficial information from the people around you, you'll see that influencing them to do whatever you desire becomes an extremely easy task!

And, they won't have even noticed that they were being gently persuaded to "reveal their hands" by your projected thoughtful character.

This exercise will eventually become a habit if your heart is in it. Habits become ingrained in the person, and you will become what you project - a more caring, more thoughtful, more empathetic person, in addition to becoming a mentalist and a phenomenal influencer.

You will gain a lot of friends and you will improve every relationship you have in your life. By giving people your 100% undivided attention, and actually listening and focusing on what they are saying, verbally and nonverbally, you will be able to give people what they want while you get what you desire.

Why not try this right now? Stop reading and go talk to your husband, wife, friend or child. Ask them to share something funny or sad that happened to them lately. Now, follow the first 3 lessons I just taught you: SMILE to make them want to share EVERYTHING with you, LISTEN in order to provide an atmosphere that invites them to TALK, and most importantly FOCUS on the way they speak. Allow them to be center stage because, remember, you took the effort to ask them a question, or otherwise initiate conversation with them, so listen and learn from what they have to say. Make them feel important, and make them feel what they are saying IS important.

While they are speaking, look at their body, their legs and hands; how do they move, what is their posture like? Look at their eyes; are they wide open? Do they look sad? What about the way they breathe? Is it calm or do they get excited? Now listen to their voice. Listen to the pace, is it slow or is it fast? Is their pitch high or low? Notice the tone and the emphasis they put on the different words in the sentences they use. What about the volume? Is it loud or do they speak really softly? What about the rhythm of their speech? Are they in a hurry to finish the story or are they taking their time?

Speech patterns, which encompass the pitch, pace, tone, rhythm and volume of the voice, give you clues about people's emotional state. Just as an example, did you know that a low and steady pitch indicates that a person is calm and in control, while a high quivering pitch indicates an anxious or insecure person?

Everything people do, whether it is subconscious, or intentional, is key to understanding what a person is communicating. Sometimes you will find that the body language or even the pitch of a person's voice is contradicting the words that they are saying.

It may not mean that they are lying, but it will indicate that there is more to their story than what they are letting on.

Perhaps you feel as though they are rushing through the story, which is why they are leaving out parts; they may not feel the omitted information is important, but it may prove to be a useful bit of knowledge for you.

It is in this situation, that you formulate your reactions to inspire them to be more forthcoming; or you could just flat out ask for further information.

Ask relevant questions, or just allow them to speak until they relax and then bring back the pertinent topic into the conversation.

Trust your instincts and if you are really paying attention to their whole being, you will be able to learn incredible amounts from even the shortest of interactions.

Can you now see how much information all this can provide? You're only on Step 3 but you already know SO MUCH about being an influential person and how to achieve an immense understanding of human behavior.

But this is only getting better; so keep reading!

Let's get back to refining your focusing skills so you will be able to extract the most information from every interaction, in every situation. As we discussed earlier, the ability to focus adroitly, is not limited for use in just one dimension of daily life but is something which is advantageous in all realms of existence, and therefore has universal application.

For the most part, if you are bad at applying focus to one area of your life, you are generally bad at focusing altogether. Here, what follows in italics, are five training exercises which will enable you to hone your Focusing skillset; they are from the 1918 book The Power of Concentration by Theron Q. Dumont. The exercises may be old, but their ability to sharpen focus has not diminished with time. I have intertwined my commentary within the exercises.

With practice, you will find that your attention will drift less when you are attempting to complete tasks and that your mind will become clearer when you need to concentrate on a specific set of tasks. If you practice these five exercises regularly and ensure that you become proficient at them, I assure you that your ability to focus in all other areas of your life will significantly improve.

Exercise 1:
Sitting Still in a Chair

Sit in a comfortable chair and see how long you can keep still. This is not as easy as it seems; you will have to make certain that all of your attention is focused on not moving while safeguarding your mind from all distractions.

Make sure that you are not making any involuntary muscular movements.

With a little practice, you will find that you are able to remain motionless for a full fifteen minutes.

At first, I advise sitting in a relaxed position for five minutes and then after you are able to keep perfectly still for this short duration, increase the time to ten minutes and then to fifteen minutes.

This is as long as it is necessary. But never strain yourself to remain stationary. You must be completely relaxed.

You will find this method of discipline is very beneficial for your thinking and for emotional and mental release. Try doing it twice a day at first and you will find that it will become easy very quickly.

Exercise 2:
Fix Gaze on Fingers or an Outstretched object.

Sit in a chair with your head up and your chin out, shoulders back.

Raise your right arm until it is level with your shoulder, pointing to your right, palm down, and fingers outstretched.

Turn your head at a right angle, 90 degrees, and fix your gaze on the tips of your outstretched fingers; if you will keep your eyes fixed on the tips, you will be able to tell if you are keeping your arm perfectly still.

Stay in this position for one minute. Do the same exercise with your left arm.

Gradually increase the time until you are able to do this for 5 minutes with each arm.

For an extra level of difficulty, totally fill a small glass of water, and grasp it by the fingers; put the arm directly in front of you.

Now fix your eyes upon the glass and try to keep the arm so steady that no movement of the water will be noticeable.

Do this first for one minute and then increase it to five minutes, per arm.

Exercise 3:
Concentrate on Opening and Closing Fists

Move your chair up to a table; place your hands upon it keeping the back of the hand on the table and clench the fists; place each thumb over the fingers of its hand.

Now fix your gaze upon the fist for a while; then, gradually extend the thumb keeping your whole attention fixed upon the act, just as if it was a matter of great importance.

Then gradually extend your first finger, then your second and so on until you open the rest. Then reverse the process, closing first the last one opened and then the rest, one by one, until you finally have the fist again in the original position with the thumb closed over the finger.

Do this exercise with the left hand. Keep up this exercise first with one hand and then the other until you have done it five times with each hand. In a few days you can increase it to ten times.

Chances are that the above exercises will at first make you "tired"; but, it is important for you to practice these monotonous exercises so you can train your attention.

It also gives you control over your muscular movement. The focus must be kept closely on each movement of the hand; if it is not, you will lose the value of the exercise.

You may think these exercises very simple and of no value, but I promise you in a short time you will notice that you have much better control over your muscular movements, carriage and demeanor; and, you will find that you have greatly improved your power of attention and can centralize your thoughts on what you do, which of course will be priceless.

Exercise 4:
When You Read

Here is another exercise to help you know whether you truly are focusing AND assimilating what you see.

Pick any type of short story and then write an abridged statement summarizing what you read. Then read an article in a newspaper, and see if you can write the essence of the article, in the fewest words possible.

Lawyers do this type of thing all the time in something called a Brief -which is a summary of all the important facts of a case, which laws apply, the issues at hand, the power of the court to hear the case etc. Documented Legal cases and issues can comprise thousands and thousands of pages, so it takes great skill to summarize all that information into just a few statements.

Law students, lawyers, legal assistants, also "brief" smaller cases from either text books, or law books of the state or nation, in a method which is similar to what I'm asking you to do. They read what is known as Case Law, law which is not legislated, but becomes a precedent after a judge makes a decision regarding the facts.and they summarize quickly, in a few sentences, or paragraph(s), the fundamentals of what they read.

So, for instance, they would just write the names of the parties involved, what the dispute was about, where it happened, what other legislative law was used in the argument of the case, if there have been other cases decided on similar issues, etc.

Journalists are taught a similar procedure; they are trained to write and extract from information the 5 W's –Who?, What?, When?, Where?, and Why?

Reading an article to get only the essentials requires the closest concentration. If you are unable to write out what you read, you will know you are weak in concentration.

Instead of writing it out you can express it orally if you wish. Go to your room and deliver it as if you were talking to someone. You will find exercises like this of the greatest value in developing concentration and learning to think discerningly.

After you have practiced a number of these simple exercises read a book for twenty minutes and then write down what you have read. The chances are that at first you will not remember very many details, but with a little practice you will be able to write a very good account of what you have read. The closer the concentration the more accurate the account will be.

It is a good idea when time is limited to read only a short sentence and then try to write it down word for word. You will find that in order to remember every word in a sentence, you must keep out every thought but that which you wish to remember. When you are able to do this, read two or more sentences and treat similarly.

Greatest success in all of the above depends largely upon cultivating, through the closest concentration, the power to image or picture what you read; upon the power, as one writer expresses it, of letting the mountains of which we hear loom before us and the rivers of which we read roll at our feet.

The practice will produce very good results if you keep it up until the habit is fixed. If you just utilize your spare time in practicing exercises like those suggested, you can gain wonderful powers of concentration.

You will find that in order to remember every word in a sentence you must keep out every thought but that which you wish to remember and this power of inhibition alone will more than compensate for the trouble of the exercise.

You can also bring this type of cultivated observation and recollection, out of the pages and into the street - when you are confronted with every situation you come across on a daily basis. Summarize in your head what you have encountered. Remember the 5 W's,

Exercise 5
Watch Concentration

Sit in a chair and place a clock with a second hand on the table. Follow the second hand with your eyes as it goes around.

Keep this up for five minutes, thinking of nothing else but the second hand, this is a very good exercise when you only have a few minutes to spare, if you are able to keep every other thought in the stream of consciousness subordinate to it.

As there is little that is particularly interesting about the second hand, it is hard to do this, but in the extra effort of will power required to make it successful, lies its value.

Remember: Always try to keep as still as possible during these exercises.

No matter what you may be doing, day or night, imagine that it is your chief object in life. Imagine you are not interested in anything else in the world but the task at hand.

Do not let your attention get away from the work you are at. Your attention will no doubt be rebellious, but control it and do not let it control you.

When once you conquer the rebellious attention you have achieved a greater victory than you can realize at the time. Many times afterwards you will be thankful you have learned to concentrate your closest attention upon the object at hand.

Let no day go by without practicing concentrating on some familiar object that is uninteresting. Never choose an interesting object, as it requires less attention.

The less interesting it is the better exercise will it be. After a little practice you will find you can center your attention on uninteresting subjects at will. The person that can concentrate can gain full control over his body and mind and be the master of his inclinations; not their slave. When you can control yourself you can control others.

You can develop a Will that will make you a giant compared with the man that lacks Will Power. Try out your Will Power in different ways until you have it under such control that just as soon as you decide to do a thing you go ahead and do it.

Never be satisfied with the "I did fairly well" spirit, but put forward your best efforts. Be satisfied with nothing else. When you have gained this you are the man you were intended to be.

Here's an exercise that you can do anyplace, anytime. It will not only train your focusing abilities, but your memory as well:

Wherever you are, look around and within two minutes try to find 5 red things that will fit in your pocket, and 5 blue objects that are too big to fit. Don't make any written etc. record of the objects.

Wait 1 minute- think about anything else during that 60 seconds. Then within 30 seconds try to remember all the objects. **Can you?**

Do you understand?

> **If i tell you i am upset about everything that is going on around me, you will probably ask me why, half listening, half wandering away in your own train of thoughts.**
> **If i tell you i am happy, you will probably not bother to know why, congratulating me and forgetting.**
> **I should rather tell you i am fine, satisfied, you will probably tell me your own issues then, for which, i will be all ears.**
> — *Sanhita Baruah*

STEP 4: UNDERSTAND

How to Be and Convey Understanding. Again I go to the sagacious motivator, Dale Carnegie, to set the tone of this chapter: **"Three-fourths of the people you will ever meet are hungering and thirsting for sympathy. Give it to them, and they will love you."**

One of the most basic skills a mentalist should have (or in fact any person should have), is an understanding of other people. What do they feel? What do they think? As I touched upon in an earlier chapter, in order to influence people you need to connect to them on a deep, rather than superficial level.

Understanding leads to sensitivity, empathy and compassion, which are fundamental qualities of the human condition. But, let us be honest here - to many people, understanding the idiosyncratic intricacies of what makes another person tick, just does not come naturally. This does not mean they are "bad" or uncaring; it just means they have not developed the skills which allow them to comprehend someone else's mental and emotional make-up.

In the seminars and workshops I conduct, I talk in detail about how to become more "attuned" to people around you, so that you can get to know them "inside and out." Believe me, this is much easier than it sounds; as long as you are motivated to learn!

In fact, you already know the first three steps towards better understanding, because they were outlined in the previous lessons: Smile, Listen intently and Focus on the messages being conveyed to you so that you can analyze and interpret them correctly.

If you have been a good student, you have already tested what you have learned on a friend, and started realizing the potential that having the mindset of a mentalist offers. For your own mental benefit, I hope that you have! Possessing mentalism skills makes this world so much more exciting!

Let me remind you of a few basics: "active" or "conscious" listening is paying focused attention, as well as showing genuine interest, openness and curiosity in what other people tell you. Once you are proficient in these skills, you can expand upon them so that you can develop a much more profound understanding of a person's outlook, character, beliefs and ideas.

In this lesson, I want to explain how to formulate questions so that they elicit the kind of answers which will help you gain a better understanding of the person with whom you are talking; instead of those which would only invoke simple "yes" or "no" responses that reveal nothing worthwhile.

Although learning to construct your questions in a Mentalistic style, involves participating in an entire course of study, I still feel it is important for me to work with you on this, here, so you will get the right 'feel' of this tool.

If you have ever correctly conducted a survey, it is the same concept. You want to ask a person for information in a way that is comfortable for them, but also construct the questions so that a simple "yes" or "no" answer would sound incomplete. Let's use an example to better understand this:

Instead of asking someone, "Do you like going to movies?" you would get a better response if you inquired, "What kind of films do you enjoy most?" The answer they provide in response to this question, will give you a glimpse into the person's interests.

If the person tells you that they enjoy comedy, you can deduce that she has a good sense of humor; if he prefers fantasy movies, you will know that they have a vivid imagination, as well as a creative streak. Based on these assumptions, you can follow up with more well-formulated questions, until you get a good sense of what makes this particular person "tick." You will have better insight to what motivates them, their personality, and reasons for their behavior.

Also, remember that it is all about the genuineness you place behind the question. While, "Do you like going to movies?" is much like asking the generic "How are you?" from last chapter, asking, "What kind of films to do you most enjoy?" is like asking about their well-being while maintaining direct eye contact and patiently waiting for their honest reply. However, asking the right kind of questions is just one of the ways to gain understanding of another. To be able to think like a mentalist requires mastering special techniques to become more sensitive and compassionate.

For instance, by imagining yourself in a similar situation as another person, by placing yourself "in another's shoes", you will grow a natural sense of empathy and understanding; by internalizing how you would react if you were in their position, you will be able to better comprehend their behaviors, and the thought patterns behind them.

Of course everyone is distinctive in certain ways and thus their responses may differ given the same situation; but, having a point of reference in your own mind as to how someone could react will help you to better understand another person's behavior.

Here's a sample list of simple questions that will help you elicit valuable information from people, and enable you to see deep into their thought processes:

- **What is important to them?**
- **What do they want?**
- **What do they like?**
- **What do they think they need?**
- **What do they think they deserve?**
- **What past memory do they want to experience again?**
- **What past memory do they want to avoid?**
- **What scares them?**
- **What excites them?**
- **What makes them happy/sad?**

Before launching into your inquisitive investigation, you must first make one important determination.

What is the subject person's state of mind? You will make this deduction utilizing the techniques given in the preceding lessons - non-verbal behavior, elements of the voice, etc. It is imperative that you make a proper assessment if you wish to extract pertinent information.

For only then will you be able to find the proper way to pick and phrase your queries.

Once you have made a general assessment as to mood and emotional state, you can then choose which questions to start with and expand upon. The questions should not be as general as is depicted above, but tailored to the person you're with. You can start with the most basic questions and then build upon each subsequent question utilizing some information gained from the answers to the questions which preceded it.

Let me give you an example situation, so you can see how this would play out. You will immediately comprehend the huge difference between a typical person asking a question, and a mentalist who uses his proficient mental abilities and mind control power to evaluate and influence someone's state of mind:

Say you meet up with your friend and you sense that she is down. An average person would ask her why she is sad! You would probably ask the same question, wouldn't you? Bad decision!

Now stop and think like a mentalist. She is obviously upset about something, but more likely than not, wouldn't want to immediately expose herself to you and open up about her problems; especially if you're not her 'best friend'.

So how can you get information to read this person, if they're standing there like a padlocked treasure chest? What is the secret then, to obtaining the key to the loot?

Well, you slowly start to adroitly "pick the lock." Introduce something about yourself when you were in a similar state of mind, so she could begin to relate to you. Once a person relates to you, they will relax and start to let their guard down. Once their guard is down, you can apply your mentalism tools, and presto! their lock will fly open faster than Houdini escaping from a straight jacket!

Here's how a situation, like described, can play out: "Hi Michelle, I'm so happy to see you again. Listen, I had such a weird experience yesterday and I'm still upset about it. (open ended statement, she has no idea what you're talking about. and maybe at this point neither do you!), but it made me think about what I want to do in my life. Did you ever have an experience like that? Something that you wish never happened, and ended up totally affecting your outlook on life?

Watch how asking the right question, without trying to directly push her into a specific state of mind, can give you beautiful, genuine answers. What you just did is touch her sadness without directly asking her why she seemed down. And even if she doesn't share the exact reason to her current melancholy mood, she'll soon explode with juicy information, like a piñata bashed open by lead baseball bat.

By telling her something about yourself, you became a compatriot in the game of life, in it together so to speak. You showed interest in her history, (remember the most important thing to a person is usually Me, Myself, and I) and you showed relatability.

Your reward will be bounteous shiny loot, to "spend" how you wish in the future.

Let's look at some more personality questions you can ask your friend. They'll help you to get to know her and should also put her in an altered state by making her dig up answers from deep within her consciousness and subconscious.

- **What was the happiest moment of your life?**
- **What role would you like to play in a Hollywood blockbuster?**
- **Achieving what goals have brought you the most joy?**
- **Do you think you know yourself well?**

These are the type of questions that will give you enough meat to bite on. You will be able to collect fascinating information from deep within her mind, and simply tap in on the information you like. Keep asking questions that will slowly guide her into divulging everything you want to know.

Don't bother with the parts of her answer where she doesn't articulate anything of depth, but when you see her become affected by her revelations, get into it as far as she will let you.

If you have conducted your initial connection and rapport techniques correctly, she will be GLAD to reveal all the juicy stuff and even happier that you are listening to it.

You must be focused and listen carefully in order to keep the conversation progressing forward seamlessly like a ticking Swiss watch. If you're getting caught off guard - it'll be very hard to get back on track. So be completely fixated on your subject and . as the title of this lesson says: UNDERSTANDING!

Introducing these questions should be a natural and continuing component of the conversation. Never ask these questions out of the blue, as it will seem as if you are interrogating her or that you have prepared and rehearsed these questions beforehand. So knowing when and how to ask these questions is extremely important.

Here's what we know by now:

When we meet a person, we will try to evaluate their current state of mind -happy, sad, angry, excited, agitated, disgusted etc.

We will start a conversation with them, yet, we will not make it 'small talk'. It is our job to create an atmosphere conducive to an open and flowing exchange of information; one where we ask open ended questions that fit in with the scenario.

Slowly and gradually we start asking specific questions we want answered and simultaneously, we keep smiling (step 1), actively listening (step 2) and completely focusing our attention on their answers, body language and non-verbal behavior (step 3)!

Influencing people's thoughts is a delicate art and it demands psychological subtleties that require a lot of patience and concentration. Don't 'think' you understand what is being communicated, be SURE you understand, because if you don't the person you're with will feel as if you're trying to manipulate him or her.

Our memories are internal representations of events. We distinguish events in our minds by linking them to our 5 senses-touch, smell, taste, sight, and hearing.

In Neuro-Linguistic Programming or NLP, our 5 senses are labelled "modalities;" they are, respectively, Kinesthetic, Olfactory, Gustatory Visual, and Auditory. When you break down the modality into small components, and qualify them, they are termed "sub-modalities".

For example, the sight modality broken down would incorporate visually related elements or qualities of an object, the individual visual distinctions attributed to the object.

the adjectives one might used to define it ex: blue, big, distorted, moving, faraway, 3-dimentional or flat looking.

These are all examples of sub-modalities. These interpretive distinctions are inextricably linked to how we represent an event in our memories. One of the best methods to discover which questions will enhance a conversation is to tap into what people remember by targeting different sub-modalities that might be attached to an experience or event.

Try the following exercise and see how much information you can gather from a friend about an object, item or place of which they are thinking.

But be sure to ask them every question in the following list, in order to ensure that you have all the information possible.

This way, you can formulate a complete picture with ease without jumping to conclusions and making an ill informed haphazard guess, which would increase the probability of getting the answer wrong.

If you ask the right questions, you should be able to determine what the friend is thinking of, within the time it takes to have asked and gotten answers to less than 20 questions.

This process is called the **Sub-modality Questionnaire**.

Ready? Let's go:

The Sub-modality Questionnaire

Ask a friend to think of an object, sound, place or any item and have them concentrate on this for a few minutes.

While they are doing this, ask them the following questions paying careful attention - actively listen and understand the answers that they provide.

Auditory Questions

- What elevation is the sound located? (Is it coming from up high, or down low?)

- Which direction is it coming from?

- It is an internal or an external sound? (Can only you hear it or can others too?)

- Is it loud or soft?

- Is it fast or slow?

- Is it high or low in pitch?

- What is its timbre (what instrument does it sound like?)

- Are there pauses or stops in the sound?

- How long does the sound last (what is its duration)?

- How unique is the sound (have you ever heard it before)?

Visual Questions

- Is the item in black and white or is it in full color?

- Is it near to you or is it far away?

- Does it appear bright or dimly lit?

- Where is it located (above, below or to the left or to the right?).

- How large is it, or how small?

- Does it have a relationship with any other object?

- It is in focus or defocused?

- Is it contained or is the image expansive?

- Is it moving or is it a still image?

- If it is in motion, is it moving at a normal pace?

- Is it 3D or 2D?

- What is the amount of contrast in the image - is it high, low or normal?

- Are you at an angle to it?

- Do you have pictures of this object and if so, which one is the most prominent?

Kinesthetic Questions.

- Where is the object located in relation to your body?
- What size is it?
- Does it have a shape?
- Does it have a color or colors?
- How intense is it?
- How steady is it? Does it feel stable or is it wobbling like jelly on a knife's edge?
- Is it still or is it moving?
- What is the duration of its occurrence?
- Is it dry or wet?
- Is it vibrating or still?
- Is it hot or cold or somewhere in between?
- Is it exerting high or low pressure?
- What is its texture?
- Is it heavy or light?
- Is it internal or external (and is it being driven by internal events or external ones?)

All of these questions can help you to understand another person's emotional state, and mindset.

These queries are regularly used in therapeutic settings to enable the therapist to comprehend a client's perspective. Make sure you learn to use a few of them and perhaps create some of your own in order to better discern the people and world around you.

A Simple Test

This is a simple test of how empathetic you are. Draw a Q on your forehead with your finger.

If you draw it with the intersecting line going towards the right you, are less empathetic than if you draw it going to the left, which is how a person would read it if they were looking at you.

Don't fret if you didn't perform this test by going to the 'left', i.e. from another person's perspective.

Only one in ten do this, but now that you are enlightened, you are a little more aware of how to see things from another person's viewpoint.

Indeed, this is such an important topic, and is the reason why I encourage my students to master it and use as many techniques as possible in order to become the best they can be.

Just think: if you can develop a deeper understanding of someone's thoughts and emotions, you will make this world a more compassionate and harmonious place! because, you will react out of knowledge, instead of emotion.

The essence of this inquisitive chapter can best be summarized by this simple phrase - "bait the hook to suit the fish." By utilizing all the previous lessons to understand the person(s) you are targeting, you will know which questions to ask to find information helpful to accomplishing your goals.

> "Personally I am very fond of strawberries and cream, but I have found that for some strange reason, fish prefer worms. So when I went fishing, I didn't think about what I wanted. I thought about what they wanted. I didn't bait the hook with strawberries and cream. Rather, I dangled a worm or grasshopper in front of the fish and said: "Wouldn't you like to have that?" Why not use the same common sense when fishing for people?"
> — *Dale Carnegie*

> **The best qualification of a Prophet is to have a good Memory.**
> -George Savile

STEP 5: MEMORIZE

In previous lessons, I talked about the importance of smiling (to get people to open up to and trust you), listening (not in order to 'hear' but in order to 'learn'), focusing (so you can notice even the smallest micro expression or nonverbal behavior) and understanding (so you don't just see all the clues but actually analyze and internalize what they mean).

Okay, after all that are we clear then on the benefits of a sharp and alert brain? Although, let me ask you this: what good is all this listening, focusing and understanding if you immediately forget everything you have learned? That's right! It's not much good at all!

That is why I want to stress the importance of committing everything you learned and observed, to memory. You may think "if I am taking all of this knowledge in, I should be able to remember it."

However, it is precisely because you are taking it so much at one time, that you will need help recalling it.

I devote entire lessons and workshops to ways of boosting your memory, because no matter what you do in life, whether you are a student cramming for exams, a worker mastering a new skill, a businessman who must remember the names of all his clients, a mother trying to remember her grocery list, or anyone else, a good memory is crucial!

Your brain is not just a storage system; good data retention also means you have a better ability to process all of the information your mind registers.

Since I cannot delve into this vast world of memory techniques in this book, I will concentrate on the basics. I hope you will begin your journey by exercising these simple methods and start developing your memory right away because these tactics can REALLY benefit you; regardless of your age, gender, or nationality.

The steps to improving your information retention are simple; but just like everything else in this guide, it does not mean that you will master them overnight or that they cannot be improved upon and sharpened, no matter how good your memory becomes.

In order to get the best from your memory, it is necessary to understand how it functions at a basic level.

Once you understand this, you can start to exploit the process in order to improve its capabilities and capture, store and retrieve information more efficiently.

There are several different layers of memory. Some things are stored in the 'Short Term memory' area of your brain, and some are stored in the 'Long Term memory' area of your brain.

Short term memory involves absorbing and retaining information in and for a matter of seconds. For example, when you arrive into a specific place and you perform Speed Tunnel Vision, as discussed in previous lessons, you want to be able to memorize as many things as you can in as short a time as possible.

However, unless you notice something very unique or peculiar while you are enacting this scan, a lot of what you remember from the place will be stored in your Short Term memory.

The Working memory is like a subset of Short Term memory. In the Working memory you internalize what you have briefly seen, and link them to representations; utilizing again, the submordality themed techniques we have spoken about before. You immediately discriminate between relevant and irrelevant information; pushing aside what is not deemed immediately important.

The Working memory stores relevant information only long enough for you to be enabled to complete tasks. It is recognized by psychologists that the maximum capacity for your Working Memory, at any particular time, is 5-7 items.

We can, however, group items up into larger units, which is how we usually remember telephone numbers (which are usually around 7 digits in length).

For example, rather than remember the number '0800294782' as one item or lots of individual numbers, we group it as 0800 294 782. This allows us to remember only three chunks of information, which is a lot easier to remember than a string of individual numbers in its entirety.

As a mentalist you must memorize many things. The cool thing about memory, though, is that even if you store data you learned in your Short-Term memory, once you exit that particular situation, your brain is not completely wiped clean of that information; the relevant elements lay dormant in your subconscious. As you become a better mentalist, it will be easier for you to recall specific information from that place if and when you need it.

This leads us to Long Term Memory. LTM is your brain's way of storing, categorizing and retrieving information that you experienced, which occurred more than a few seconds in the past. When tapping into the Long Term memory, elements that were lying dormant, in the Working memory portion of the brain, or the subconscious, can be brought up to the surface, or consciousness.

There are two different parts to LTM. The memories that are available to the consciousness are called Declarative memories; those are then divided into two more compartments, one in which specific events are retained, or Episodic memory, and the other where all general knowledge is stored, or Semantic memory.

Then there is the second part of LTM which involves retaining information pertaining to HOW to do things- like driving a car, or riding a bike; this is called Procedural memory.

If, for instance, you need to remember something like a friend or family member's birthday, you will be more inclined to store that information in the relative section of the Long-Term memory area as this is data that you would probably deem relevant. Relevant information tends to be easier to access.

What is important to recognize is that Memory does not function like a video recorder or a hard drive capturing and recording every aspect of our lives; it, as previously mentioned, is an associative process. Information is filtered and linked to things which have been already stored on previous occasions.

Therefore, in order to make the most of your memory, you need to develop a system by which you can easily associate any new information to any old information; thus, in effect, making more and more information relevant. Luckily for us, we have the perfect tool to accomplish this: narrative. Narrative, or storytelling, allows us to take objects, people and concepts, and combine them to create unlimited possibilities.

Try the next exercise to get the flavor of this...

Read through the following list of words:

1. Chicken
2. Handbag
3. Airplane
4. Salmon
5. Tree
6. Sword
7. Necklace
8. Dress
9. Sheep
10. Emperor
11. Chips
12. Milkshake
13. Book
14. Cell
15. Transmitter
16. Headphones
17. Mouse
18. Wire
19. Camera
20. Switch

Now, I would like you to time yourself and take only ONE minute to try to commit these words, in order, to memory. Once you have done this (or attempted to do this), put down this book and write them on a piece of paper, in order, from 1 to 20. Any items which you cannot remember leave blank.

Go now!

My guess is that you were able to remember perhaps the first 4-5 of the list, and then the next ten were hazy followed by a resurgence of memory at the end - with the last four perhaps making a re-appearance into consciousness.

These lapses are due to cognitive biases within our brain; one of which is called the Primacy Effect (which states that we have a tendency to remember information that is first presented to us) and one called the Recency Effect (we remember the information most recently seen).

Most probably, you looked over the list of items in order, several times, and tried to burn the sequence into your memory. With this fairly poor strategy in place, you are essentially only relying on the safety net of cognitive or conscious mental efforts, to save you from not remembering any information at all.

With just a little change, you can allow this list to skip from your Working memory (which only holds onto information for a matter of seconds) into your Long Term memory.

In order for this storage transition to occur, you have to translate the information from your Working memory into your Long Term memory, by using language the Long Term memory finds appealing.

This "translation" usually involves incorporating experiences with different elements of our 5 senses. Once again we bring to the forefront the NLP theory of submodalities. We are basically talking about how events are coupled with emotions invoked by sight, sound, smell, taste and touch. If you construct a narrative around the 20 item list, and link each individual one with a component of your 5 senses, most likely an emotion will be elicited from this joining. This will enable you to remember the items much more clearly and with relative ease; in comparison, say, to simply trying to force them from your Working memory.

So how do you coax emotion into this scenario? You may have been asked the question before, "are you more right-brain dominant (creative, expressive, intuitive, artistic etc.), or left brain dominant (logical, mathematical, critical in thinking and reasoning etc.)"? Well, for all of our purposes, I want you to be ambidextrous brain dominant! Knowing how to draw from both sides!

For this exercise, you're going to tap into the right side; the more creative and outrageous the narrative is, the more likely you will compel some time of emotional response; and therefore, the more likely you will be to remember the elements on your list, in the order in which they occurred.

Here is an example of a narrative I would use to remember the 20 items written previously:

*On my way to work this morning I saw a **<u>Chicken</u>** with a lime green **<u>Handbag</u>** walking along the sidewalk. This was so bizarre that I almost crashed into an **<u>Airplane</u>** engine that was being transported to the industrial site near my work. I focused on getting to work and quickly put this experience out of my mind.*

*For lunch, I had some **<u>Salmon</u>** and sat under a **<u>Tree</u>** in the parking lot. I had a very sharp knife to eat my meal; it was like a polished **<u>Sword</u>** and reminded me of a shiny **<u>Necklace</u>** or fancy **<u>Dress</u>** that sparkled and shimmered. I didn't go to lunch with any other people as I did not want to be considered a **<u>Sheep</u>**. I am my own **<u>Emperor</u>**.*

*All the work canteen serves is **<u>Chips</u>** with **<u>Milkshake</u>**. I would rather sit outside and read a **<u>Book</u>**. However, the **<u>Cell</u>** phone **<u>Transmitter</u>** next to the parking lot makes an awful hum when I sit out there so I usually wear **<u>Headphones</u>** and listen to some music on my MP3 player.*

*The other day I saw a huge blue **<u>Mouse</u>** outside while I was eating my lunch. At first I thought it was a giant **<u>Cable</u>** or root coming out of the ground but it moved very quickly. I rushed to grab my **<u>Camera</u>** to take a photo of it, but the **<u>Switch</u>** gave me an electric shock and I dropped it on the ground.*

OK, there is no way I am going to win any awards for my creative writing ability, but you get the point. As an exercise, create your own story around these twenty words.

It is important that every story is uniquely yours, as you are the only one with your brain and experiences, and therefore will be the only one to determine the associations best remembered. See how imaginative you can be.

If you are having problems handling a list of 20, you might want to reduce the number of items to remember, and then gradually build the list back up.

If you get stuck creating your story, try this as an easier exercise: Instead of writing a shopping list this week, try and construct a story with your groceries; upon your return from the store, give a point for every item remembered. Then keep a score sheet and see if the number of items remembered increases with time. You might surprise yourself as to how fast you excel at the task.

Other recollection techniques employ ideas such as utilizing the image of a familiar place or journey (called Memory Palaces or a Memory Journey); this is where you place objects or representations of items that you wish to remember along a familiar route or in a familiar place within your mind.

To use a Memory Palace, choose a very familiar location (such as your route to work, or the layout of your home) and place objects which cue particular themes or ideas, within your mental imagery of this route.

For example, if you wanted to remember presidents of the United States, you would ascribe a characteristic of each president to an object within your home, and then virtually walk through your house encountering all of these objects at a later date.

This method has been used over and over again by world class memory champions to remember an entire plethora of information- from telephone numbers to multiple decks of cards, and is extremely effective! So, pick something you want to remember and practice! The most important thing is to practice your new skills whenever you get the opportunity.

In this quick overview, I will be discussing several more ways of boosting your memory; they go hand-in-hand. In other words, for the maximum effect, you should practice them together.

The first one is providing nourishment to the brain with what you eat - like Omega 3 fatty acids found in fatty fish, which have been proven to enhance cognitive function; and to indulge in delicious dark chocolate! which stimulates the production of the brain chemical dopamine - it enables learning and memory and keeps the brain sharp.

The second is exercising your brain so it stays supple and agile. There are two courses of action someone can take to accomplish the latter; the first is to get a healthy dose of physical exercise, which pumps oxygen-rich blood to the brain and benefits the hippocampus, a brain structure that is important for data interpretation and retention, and the second is a mental workout such as brain teasers, word games, Rubik's cube, Sudoku, etc.

You can do other fun things like go to a museum and once you arrive home write down all the paintings you had seen, and the order in which you saw them. Or you pick a song you like but don't know lyrics to - and see how fast you can learn them. These exercises will keep your brain active and alert, which, in turn, will be more conducive to having a great memory.

Another very effective method is a technique called mnemonics. In a nutshell, mnemonics work by linking pieces of known information in your mind with something new that you've just learned. The fun part of this approach is that it is based on word play, so people of all ages will enjoy practicing it!

I will give you one concrete example which uses something called an acronym. Acronyms are words, or a word, formed from the first letters of each of the words in a phrase. Sound confusing? It's really not. They help condense a list or a complicated word pattern by making it into something far more simple, so that your memory is triggered by easy cues.

Let's say you want to memorize all the colors of the rainbow. All you have to remember is the name Roy G. Biv, who is not actually a real person, but a clever acronym for the color sequence of the rainbow: Red, Orange, Yellow, Green, Blue, Indigo, and Violet.Get it? It's fun, isn't it? And the best thing is that similarly structured acronyms will help you memorize subjects like Astronomy, Geography, Mathematics, enhance name re-call etc.

A more common word that some may not even realize is an acronym is SCUBA-which stands for Self Contained Underwater Breathing Apparatus.

Now try this: Think of a grocery list; lets say, ten items: Potatoes, apples, hot dogs, cinnamon, cookies, wine, honey, bread, French fries, Worcester sauce.

Now, think of a sentence where the first letter of every word starts with something on your list. For Instance: Patty Attends Her Cooking Class With Her Best Friend Weekly.

It doesn't necessary have to be a grammatically correct sentence, it just has to be something you will remember. I also encourage my students to develop their own Major Mnemonic System by using words that are close to their hearts and incorporating them into a guide sheet for what they need to memorize.

They create a list of words numbered 1-100, and then by associations, my students are able to memorize 100 different things and recall them at any time!

How do they do that? This system works by converting numbers into consonant sounds, then into words by adding vowels.

It relies on the principle that images can be remembered more easily than numbers. That makes sense to you, right? Now, by having a different word represent each one of the numbers from 1 to 100, they're able to create an instant association from the word to what they need to remember.

I know it sounds complicated but once you get the feel for it, this exercise will become second nature to you!

If you read a list of 100 items to me, I will 'associate' each item with the correspondent word I have for that slot, and will be able to recite all the elements of the list top to bottom and bottom to top! If you decide that you want to have the powers of a professional mentalist, you too will be able to do this! And I promise, it is much easier than you think.

There are a lot of memory techniques out there so don't be discouraged if the ones that I have already mentioned don't seem to work for you. And do not be afraid to practice learning new material with every opportunity you get. The human capacity for memory is effectively infinite. You can never run out of room.

So do yourself and your brain a favor! Start exploring and learning new ways to improve your memory. That is one superpower we all can use because it makes us much smarter and since we remember what we have to do on a daily basis far more easily, that leads to less stress!

> **It's very important that we relearn the art of resting and relaxing. Not only does it help prevent the onset of many illnesses that develop through chronic tension and worrying; it allows us to clear our minds, focus and find creative solutions to problems.**
> *-Thich Nhat Hanh*

STEP 6: RELAX

Chill Out! This is one major important lesson, and is related back to the steps where we spoke about meditation and clearing the mind. We encountered in the last chapter the idea of having less stress due to a better memory. Here we'll discuss the opposite side of the spectrum - having a better memory due to less stress.

You will not be able to focus; you will not be able to absorb, interpret and retain data, if stressful hormones are pulsing through you veins.

Adrenaline, the fight or flight hormone, pumps blood and therefore oxygenation to the major muscles, heart and lungs to prepare for one of the two mentioned scenarios - duke it out, or run for the dunes. It increases your heart rate, your blood pressure, your pulse rate, and your glucose and lipid levels. What it doesn't usually raise, is your mental acuity.

With all this attention being paid to your other organs, your brain functions decrease sharply. The brain centers governing reason and logic, memory and conscious thought are basically being ignored in favor of those that control autonomic reactions. So the parts of the brain most important to our discussions, are receiving less blood and therefore less oxygen. In a nutshell, stress makes you stupid.

Dr. Steven Stein and his company Multi-Health Systems have conducted many studies on how stress also effects what is known as EQ, Emotional Intelligence.

EQ is a phrase which was coined in the mid 1990's by Daniel Goldmen's book of the same name, and a 1995 TIME magazine cover article entitled "The EQ Factor" by Nancy Gibbs.

As referenced in these publications, the concept refers to the capability to interpret situations, others feelings, and the ability to convey or communicate your own feelings, desires and needs.

Dr. Stein, has published his findings on the stress EQ correlation, and his results are extraordinarily pertinent to our discussions, here. He has found that: "A strong emotional intelligence can help build positive relationships. and improve performance.

But if stress prevents us from being aware of and controlling our emotions, getting along with others, adapting to changes, and maintaining a positive mood, then our EI is going to suffer. In fact, it has been scientifically demonstrated that emotional intelligence is actually more important in predicting success . than IQ (cognitive intelligence)."

- He further elaborated on his conclusions by stating that stress:

- Affects decision-making, making us too impulsive.

- Forces us to make mistakes.

- Causes us to ignore cues.

- Interferes with relationships.

- Lowers productivity.

We all know that stress is bad for our health, but as you can now see, for a Mentalist, stress is truly public and private enemy #1. So what weapon do you need to fight the enemy?

Learn to control your body and mind, by learning to - relax.

Yes you heard me right - **<u>RELAX</u>**.

Forgotten what that is?

Let me remind you "to release or bring relief from the effects of tension, anxiety, etc."

It's hard to believe that we actually need to be taught to unwind, but for must of us, this technologically advanced society hasn't made our lives any more carefree.

Remember the pandemic Multitasking Influenza from our first chapters? Well, I'm going to inoculate you from its effects; you and your adrenal glands are going to thank me. Promise.

You may still be wondering how relaxation techniques can boost your mental powers and help you to influence people. At first thought you may think that "letting go" may actually dull your senses and state of awareness; however, that would be a wrong assumption.

As we touched upon before, not only is chronic tension a detriment to your mental functions and stamina, it is also a contributing factor to several serious medical conditions, including heart disease and strokes.

Additionally, if you cannot find any relief from strain, you will likely experience anxiety, headaches, insomnia, dizziness and other disturbances on a consistent basis, throughout your life. None of this is conducive to living a happy fulfilled existence, much less promoting the ability for beneficial interactions and communications.

All of us live with varying degrees of consternation, whether it's related to work, school, relationships, or any other source. The important thing, though, is to learn to reduce the stress level as much as possible, so that it does not damage our physical and mental health or impair our lives.

Mental relaxation is by far the best antidote. It simultaneously releases toxic tension from our mind and body, while at the same time promotes more energy, vitality and inner-strength.

Unfortunately, many people think that taking time off is time sorely wasted time. This couldn't, of course, be further from the truth. Time taken off contributes to better and more efficient usage of time "on".

If you are one of those people who never take a few minutes to calm down and relax, I hope that these tips will inspire you to give it a try!

I want to share with you a relaxation technique that has proven very effective, for me. I practice it on a daily basis, and I hope you will be able to use it in your daily life as well. Basically it consists of deep and slow breathing in conjunction with visualization.

However, the breathing will only become tension releasing if you first clear your mind of all distractions. Yes, I know clearing your mind of all distractions without falling asleep is easier said than done. Still, I want to assure you that with a little bit of effort on your part, this goal can be achieved!

So if I need to choose one easy way from the arsenal of methods I use, I recommend exerting a bit of influence over your mind. Imagine a soothing color - pure, with no imperfections. Close your eyes take a deep breath in and think to yourself: right now, my brain is as clean and calm as the color I am seeing.

Remember that influence is a gigantic word. Influence is "the capacity to be a compelling force on the character, development, or behavior of someone or something; or, the ability to produce effects on the actions, behavior, or opinions, of others."

❦❦ A mentalist must learn to influence inside and out.

What do I mean by saying "Inside and Out?"

Very simply: You must learn to be strong and effective within your own self. You need to learn how to influence YOURSELF as much as you influence OTHERS.

You must compel yourself to become more relaxed and manipulate your mind to be free from agitation, excitement, or disturbance.

Conjuring up a peaceful image, a beautiful landscape of scenery for example, will also help you breathe calmly while keeping disruptive thoughts away from your mind.

Once you see that scenery in your mind, you are going to want to take it all in.

Imagine you have actually stepped foot into that image. See every beautiful detail, feel the earth under your feet, smell the aroma of the air and totally immerse yourself inside of it; become one with it. Now clear your mind of anything but that beautiful panorama.

Progressive Relaxation

The very idea of deliberately relaxing can sometimes make people tense up as they fear they will not be able to do it. The most important thing to remember is that relaxing is a natural state for the body to adopt. In fact, it is the simplest and most pleasurable state for the body to be in. Most people are only truly relaxed when they are asleep and spend all of their waking hours in a state of perpetual tension. Using the following techniques, I shall teach you how to take a break from the stresses and strains of daily life and show you how to be able to take a 20 minute breather to refresh yourself.

One of the most powerful ways to unwind is by using something called Progressive relaxation. I would like you to read the following script to yourself (or better yet, get a friend to do it) and follow all of its instructions.

The total allocation of time dedicated to reading it should be about twenty minutes -so don't rush it. Remember, the goal of this is to ensure that you are completely and utterly relaxed. Once you have recorded the script (or have asked someone to read it to you) the exercise can be done with closed eyes; but for now, just follow the instructions with your eyes open, preferably in a comfortable chair.

Make sure you do this with an alarm set if you need to be somewhere shortly after, as you may find yourself drifting to sleep.

Progressive Muscle Relaxation script

This meditation and visualisation exercise will help to remove negative emotions from your body, it can be done at any time and should take between five and ten minutes.

Find yourself a quiet place where you will not be disturbed, and turn off anything that might distract you, including your phone, the television and the radio. This exercise is best done in silence.

Sit in a comfortable cross-legged position. If you are not used to sitting in this way then you can lie down instead. The important thing is to be comfortable.

This is an exercise based on the ideas of visualisation of energy and the healing power of the Sun. I will ask you to imagine healing energy flowing from the Sun and through your body. If you feel uncomfortable or unsure at any time, then you can simply relax and focus on your breathing. A good idea will be to record yourself reading this script, or to find my own recorded scripts online.

Let's begin.

Close your eyes and slowly bring your attention to your thoughts. Try and observe your thoughts without judging them as good or bad, simply watch as new thoughts appear in your mind and let them pass through and dissipate. Try not to become attached to your thoughts but instead be like an outside observer, merely watching your thoughts arise and change.

As new thoughts arise simply observe them without judgement. If you become distracted then bring your attention back to observing your thoughts.

Now bring your attention to your breath. Close your mouth and breathe deeply and naturally through your nose.

As you breathe in deeply, feel the air rushing through your nose, notice the sensations down your throat, feel your chest rise as the air flows into your lungs.

As you breathe out fully, feel your chest relax as the air pushes back out of your throat and through your nose.

Notice the muscles in your body move as you breathe in and out, try and feel every little sensation that you feel as you breathe.

Breathe in

And out

Breathe in

And out

Now, imagine a bright, small Sun floating above your head. Imagine the Sun's rays and heat washing down over you. Feel the warmth of the Sun.

As the rays and heat of the Sun spread down onto your body, fell the energy gently entering the top of your head, and slowly spreading down through your body.

Feel this healing, warm energy spreading down through your head, and gently down through your neck.

Feel the energy spread down to your chest and out into your shoulders. Imagine the warmth spreading through your shoulders and down your arms, all the way to the tips of your fingers.

Bring your attention back to the Sun and feel the warm, healing energy again flowing through your head and down through your chest and the core of your body, spreading downwards to the base of your body. Feel the energy spreading into your legs. Feel it gently spread warmth all the way down to your toes.

Feel the warm and healing energy flowing through your entire body. Let the energy come from the Sun above your head, into the top of your head, and all the way through your body and out through your fingers and toes. Imagine the energy gently flowing through your body.

Imagine that as the warm, healing energy flows through you it is also spreading a bright light, feel the light healing your body and spreading wellbeing throughout.

As this healing light flows through your body feel it picking up any negativity, any pain, and pushing this negative energy out of your fingers and toes. Feel the negative energy leaving your body. Imagine the negativity as small black spots in the otherwise pure white light. Feel the light energy push these black spots out of your fingers and toes.

Let the energy flow through you, cleansing you of negative energy and emotions. As the negativity is washed away feel the light growing in strength within you, becoming brighter, purer and warmer, until it is a bright white healing light flowing through your entire body.

Feel the bright white light shining through your entire body and filling you with positive energy and emotions.

Let the bright healing energy flow from the top of your bed all the way through your body, spreading wellbeing through you.

Breathe in

And out

Feel the energy flowing from the Sun above your head through your head, chest, shoulders, arms, fingers legs and toes. Feel it fill every part of you with bright and positive energy and emotions.

Focus on these positive emotions of wellbeing and peace. Feel content to sit in the healing light of the Sun.

Now the Sun is slowly beginning to fade. As it fades imagine the bright energy flowing out of your fingers and toes, leaving behind only positivity and wellbeing.

Let the Sun slowly fade away and the energy flowing through you gently dissipate through your fingers and toes. Your body has now been cleansed of negativity, leaving you with a feeling of wellbeing and contentedness.

As the energy fades, bring your attention back to your breath. Breathe in and out deeply through your nose as before.

Breathe in deeply

Breathe out, letting any lingering negativity flow out with your breath.

Breathe in

And out

Bring your attention back to the sensations in your body. Feel your muscles move as you breathe. Feel the air flow through your nose, throat and chest.

Now gently come back to the world. Focus on the feelings of wellbeing throughout your body.

Now gently open your eyes.

Smile.

Give thanks to yourself for cleansing your body of negativity in this way. Take a minute or two more to relax, and gently observe your inner feelings of wellbeing and peace. If you have time and you feel sleepy then take a nap. When you awake you will be filled with feelings of wellbeing and peace.

Take a Power Nap

If you do find yourself falling asleep when you perform the above Progressive relaxation exercise, this is a clear indication that you are probably sleep deprived. If this is the case, then one of the best ways to allow your body to feel revitalized is to take a Power nap.

A Power nap is a sleep of a sufficiently short duration, not exceeding thirty minutes from the point you drift off. You will only enter sleep stages 1 and 2, thus avoiding the deeper REM sleeps of a full sleep cycle; which when interrupted, will leave you feeling disorientated and groggy or suffering from what is termed "sleep inertia"- this will result in you being in a state worse off than you were before the nap.

Power napping has a host of positive benefits; studies support its powerful affects on the body and mind.

One such study conducted in the University of Düsseldorf, found that after only 6 minutes of sleep, a person's memory recall reached the superior level -suggesting that while asleep for this short duration, the mind consolidates stimuli gathered when alert, processes it, and has it available for access upon awakening.

Another study conducted by a University of Pennsylvania School of Medicine professor, David F. Dinges, for the benefit of NASA (the National Aeronautics and Space Administration of the United States) concluded that naps not only improve many kinds of memory functions, but in some cases are as good as a full night of sleep for some types of memory performance.

So, for any given Power napping period, provide yourself with a window of no more than forty-five minutes total - this will give you up to fifteen minutes to fall asleep fully.

If you have timed this process properly, when you wake up, you will find that you are refreshed and ready for work again.

However, if you mistimed it (napped for more than 30 minutes) you may find it difficult to wake up and may suffer from sleep inertia. Practice this technique before relying on it, because it is highly individual and effects people in different ways.

This, by the way, is the theory behind the Spanish practice of a siesta; having a sleep in the middle of the afternoon helps boost performance for the remainder of the day. It also helps to avoid the heat of the mid-day sun, which can be physically and mentally draining.

Power napping has been shown to be so important, that several major corporations such as Google now have sleep centers for their staff - allowing them to take a power nap, on company time, in order to increase their overall productivity. This has been just a quick overview, but I hope that you will decide to study the world of relaxation techniques in the near future.

I will further delve into the exploration of how to relax in my upcoming my new book tentatively titled "The Mentalist's Meditation Concepts";

or perhaps I might have the pleasure to see you in my full program one day, where I will guide you through breathing and relaxation methodologies, step by step.

Some of the most important things to take away from this chapter are the following:

Focus on the imagery you have created as a process to clear your mind. Remember, clearing your mind is not an idle process!

This means that you should be aware of each movement and every breath. Be acutely aware of what you are doing and how your body and mind responds to it; feel the muscles relax, pay attention to the relief you find when the tension from your neck and shoulders begin to melt away.

Do not miss one moment of experiencing the blissful relaxation enveloping you. Every step of this should be done mindfully and intensely.

Remember your goal is a balanced mind, body and soul. By doing these exercises you are elevating your mental prowess. Just as your body and soul need sleep, your mind needs conscious relaxation.

Here is the basic truth: **Relaxation is an inseparable part of being a successful mentalist.**

When you're stressed you will not be able to smile a genuine **smile** and attract people to you.

When you're stressed you won't be able to create a **real connection** to the people you're with and seek to know better.

When you're stressed you won't be able to **listen and concentrate**, and respond adequately to what people say.

When you're stressed there is no way you will be able to **focus, memorize and internalize** what is happening around you.

❦ So in summary, as I said before – STRESS MAKES YOU STUPID.

Relaxation through breathing and imagery is one of the most powerful weapons against stress!

Use it!

> **Nothing can STOP the man with the right mental attitude from achieving his goal;
> nothing on earth can HELP the man with the wrong mental attitude.**
> *-Thomas Jefferson*

STEP 7: ATTITUDE

Do you need an attitude adjustment? I know what you must be thinking: the word "attitude" is so broad and general that it needs to be narrowed down and understood better. It could be a life-altering statement, a coming of age requirement or just a situational objective. There is so much that could be taken from just one word that the possible meanings are endless.

So to begin lets look at some interpretations of the word:

An online dictionary defines attitude as

1. *Manner, disposition, feeling, position, etc., with regard to a person or thing; tendency or orientation, especially of the mind: a negative attitude; group attitudes.*

2. Position or posture of the body appropriate to or expressive of an action, emotion, etc.: a threatening attitude; a relaxed attitude."

Merriam Webster puts it more simply:

1. The way you think and feel about someone or something.

2. A feeling or way of thinking that affects a person's behavior.

Psychologists define attitude as:

"An expression of favor or disfavor toward a person, place, thing, or event (the attitude object)."

It is an attitude of curiosity that compelled you to acquire this Book and an attitude of determination that made you read it thus far. Everything in your life is controlled by the attitude with which you approach it.

So here's what I mean by the word:

For the mentalist, "attitude" is the kind of thought process and behavior that is a source of positive and uplifting energy; it not only fills YOU, but also spreads to others.

Attitude is a philosophy of approaching life with optimism and confidence, thus enabling you to control your life and influence everyone around you in a positive way!

I know that it is not an easy mindset to adopt because, let's face it, life is sometimes full of hardships. However, here's the thing: having a positive outlook will not only make you more resilient, but it will also help you face challenges better. It's all.a matter of attitude.

In case you are wondering why a positive mindset is so important, it is because your attitude determines how successful you are in your career and in your relationships. In fact, studies have shown that a positive mindset will be more likely to bring positive results in all realms, because optimism generates good energy, which, in turn, makes you try harder to succeed.

On the other hand, if you have a negative attitude and are sure that you will fail at an undertaking, chances are you won't even try. This is what we call a "self-fulfilling prophecy."

How do you think people "move mountains" and do what others say is impossible? It is not because a magical wand was waved and the road was paved with gold for them, or they were handed a how-to manual.

Rather, greatness is in many cases bred under the worst of circumstances; it is all up to the person confronting the insurmountable to find the proper path to ensure a successful climb, and ultimately imbed their flag at the summit.

Usually, the process of confronting the "impossible" is wrought with negativity from the outside world and only lauded upon success.

The climb upward is often hindered by rocks thrown from the most unexpected of people; which is exactly why you need to create your own destiny, your own happiness and your own positivity. If you believe in something, then keep that positive energy flowing toward it, because a lot of the time, you will find it is really all up to you!

What do you see when you look at this picture?

There are actually two words displayed here. Some will see one word and not the other; some will see both.

Which word you see, or which word you see first, is a good indication of how you view the world. For the record the two words are "**victory**" and "**defeat**".

It actually took quite a long time for me to see the word "defeat." I had to really scrutinize the image. How about you?

An optimistic frame of mind should not depend upon how good or bad the environment around you may appear to others. It's all a matter of your perspective; if the glass is half full instead of half empty, then you clearly have a positive attitude.

It also has to do a lot with relativity.and I don't mean Einstein's theory of relativity, but rather how things seem in relation to one another. For instance, if you believe that you are poor, think of those who are much worse off than you and try to help them any way you can. This will not only help their situation, but it will also help you feel better about yourself - which in turn will increase your positiveness in general.

In order to help put yourself in an affirmative mindset, when you get up tomorrow morning, before you do anything else, I would like for you to do this exercise: Stand in front of a mirror and say five positive things about yourself.

These statements do not have to be complicated; you just have to truly feel them. For instance, you could say, "You are a strong, confident person," or "You are a caring person," or "You are a great musician." Whatever it is that makes you feel positively about yourself, I want you to proclaim it in the mirror.

Do this every day, either with the same complements or add new ones as you go along. This should put you in a positive frame of mind first thing in the morning, which will start your day off right!

In my lectures, I explain how techniques like Neuro-linguistic programming can help modify your thoughts and behavior. But before you start practicing these methods, you have to "re-program" your mind. A good way to illustrate this "relativity" point is this proverb: "I felt sorry for myself because I had no shoes -- until I met a man who had no feet." Do you see what I mean? When you look at life, you have to be part philosopher and part psychologist because only by putting things into the right perspective can you generate a positive attitude.

Perspective

This perspective component of attitude is how to appreciate yourself and the people around you in your daily life.

Remember - how something appears is always a matter of perspective:

My only brother, Nimrod, was killed in battle at the age of 28, while on reserve duty as a Sergeant Major. The day they knocked on my door to bring me the message about his falling, was the day my life changed completely.

A few years have now passed since I last saw my brother and hugged him – but his memory still burns brightly in my mind. He had an electrifying look with an old wise soul and his presence in my life showed me the way so many times. Everything there is to know about me, he knew; my deepest secrets, my worst nightmares, my biggest passions - everything. When he died I wrote a song. You see everybody writes songs about how much they miss their loved ones once they are gone. But there was a unique spin to my song; in my song I wrote what the person who died writes to the person who is still alive! I called the song "Now that I am dead."

I want to share the chorus line, because I believe it will help understand this lesson a bit better:

> *Now that I am dead*
>
> *It's all so clear in my head*
>
> *To get perspective*
>
> *You must first pass away*
>
> *Only then you realize*
>
> *How life passed you by*
>
> *What a shame you realize it*
>
> *Only when you die*

The reason to live a life with this type of attitude is not only to avoid feelings of guilt and regret when it's too late, but more importantly, to live a life to be proud of. As you learn the Mentalist steps of influencing, you should always keep in mind to treat people with kindness. The steps you take throughout this journey will make the people around you know their true value to you. And the biggest gift of it all - is that by following these guidelines it will also open others up to do the same to you!

Let's take a closer look: Everyone has someone in their life that makes them feel good about themselves whenever they are around them; someone who has the mentioned Mentalist qualities, by nature. Take a moment to think about who that person is in your life.

Maybe you're lucky and there's more than one. Do they possess some kind of super power? The answer is both YES and no - because it is a super power we can all access if we choose to! This book should bring you closer to achieving this goal faster. Now ask yourself: **What do these "feel good" people do to make us feel so loved and appreciated?**

Perhaps it is their naturally positive attitude and infectious smile they bring everywhere. Maybe it's their excitement and enthusiasm to simply spend time with you. Or, that they are fully "present" when with you and are truly curious about what's going on with you and your life; and, they remember things that you've told them - whether it be events in the present or past, things about your family, or the date of your birthday.

Conceivably it could be because they put in the effort to keep communication going even when they are busy with their own life - and so on. Every one of us has someone like this in their life – they are a true pleasure to be around and to call a friend.

A good mentalist knows how to adopt these practices so that he too can light up other people's lives, even if that person is a complete stranger. That means your thoughts have to be a lot less directed inward and a lot more concentrated outward. In this day in age, it seems that people are almost encouraged to be narcissists.

It seems that everyone is their own celebrity - with their Facebook Page, their Twitter Account, their blog, their public sharing of both failures and successes. Narcissism is the antithesis of a quality a mentalist should possess. The simplest and best method to achieving the 'right attitude' is to follow **"The Golden Rule"**:

"Treat Others The Way You Yourself Would Like to be Treated."

Perhaps these concepts seem overly saccharine to you, but the truth is – they work! I assure you nothing bad can happen. Taking time to appreciate everyone around you is a meaningful legacy you can leave behind and it is infectious. This is your chance to do it – while there's still time!

Believe it or not - I think that it is my attitude that brought me the success I have.

I became my statements.

I started by looking in the mirror and telling myself that I can do this or that. that my smile is beautiful.that my memory is phenomenal. I was programming myself to believe in the person I was looking at! **Me!**

You can't imagine how important it is to actually believe in you.

Change the word YOU and instead say your FULL name. Do this out loud right now!

Say three times: "I believe in (your full name)", then louder **"I believe in (your full name)"** and now scream it out loud so the person in the other room will come and check what the heck is going on: <u>**"I BELIEVE IN (YOUR FULL NAME)!"**</u>

Don't be shy! If you can't do this exercise then you have a long way to go in order to achieve your goal of becoming an influencing mentalist. But if you follow my exercise, it means you're half way there! Congratulations!

Here are some examples of a dramatic mindset change taken from a superb book <u>The Seven Habits of Highly Effective People</u> by **Stephen Covey.** The first is a humorous example and the second brings forward a little more introspection.

Both illustrate how an attitude of an open mind allows us to see necessary relevant information which can alter our perspectives on a situation, and how our attitude toward events can affect our overall outlook on life and the world in general.

First Scenario

Two battleships assigned to the training squadron had been at sea on manoeuvres in heavy weather for several days.

I was serving on the lead battleship and was on watch on the bridge as night fell. The visibility was poor with patchy fog, so the captain remained on the bridge keeping an eye on all activities. Shortly after dark, the lookout on the wing of the bridge reported, "Light, bearing on the starboard bow."

"Is it steady or moving astern?" the captain called out. Lookout replied, "Steady, captain," which meant we were on a dangerous collision course with that ship.

The captain then called to the signal man, "Signal that ship: We are on a collision course, advise you change course 20 degrees."

Back came a signal, "Advisable for you to change course 20 degrees." The captain said, "Send: I'm a captain, change course 20 degrees."

"I'm a seaman second class," came the reply.

"You had better change course 20 degrees."

By that time, the captain was furious. He spat out, "Send: I'm a battleship. Change course 20 degrees."

Back came the flashing light, "I'm a lighthouse."

We changed course.

Second Scenario

Try to imagine you are at the station. While you're waiting for the next train, you think of some biscuits you've got in your bag.

You patiently search for an available seat so you can sit down and enjoy your biscuits. Finally, you find a seat next to a man.

You reach down into your bag and pull out your pack of biscuits. As you do so, you notice that the man starts watching you intensely. He stares as you open the pack and his eyes follow your hand as you pick up the biscuit and eat it. Just then he reaches over and takes one of your biscuits from the pack, and eats it! Actually, you're at a loss for words. Not only does he take one biscuit, but he also alternates eating them with you.

Now, what's your immediate impression of this guy? Crazy? Greedy? He gets on your nerves? Can you imagine the words you might use to describe this man? Meanwhile, you both continue eating the biscuits until there's just one left.

To your surprise, the man reaches over and takes it. But then he does something unexpected. He breaks it in half, and gives half to you. After he's finished with his half he gets up, and without a word, he leaves.

You think to yourself, "Did this really happen?" You're left sitting there dumbfounded and still hungry.

So you try to find a kiosk and buy another pack of biscuits. You then return to your seat and begin opening your new pack of biscuits when you glance down into your bag. Sitting there in your bag is your original pack of biscuits - still unopened.

Only then do you realize that when you reached down earlier, you had reached into the other man's bag, and grabbed his pack of biscuits by mistake.

Now what do you think of the man? Generous? Tolerant? You've just experienced a profound paradigm shift. You're seeing things from a new point of view. Is it time to change your point of view?

Both of these examples demonstrate a drastic change of attitude due to a dramatic change in paradigm or perspective. So the next time you find your emotions running away with you, try and see a bigger picture and get control of an attitude that can sometimes cloud what is actually happening and your reaction to it. You will find the world is a much better more understanding place if you do!

In the meantime, remember this wonderful quote by Winston Churchill:

> **Attitude is a LITTLE thing that makes a BIG difference.**

Each morning when I open my eyes I say to myself: I, not events, have the power to make me happy or unhappy today. I can choose which it shall be. Yesterday is dead, tomorrow hasn't arrived yet. I have just one day, today, and I'm going to be happy in it.

- Groucho Marx

STEP 8: BE HAPPY

Do you want to be happy? Of course you do! The pursuit of happiness is a major part of our life's journey and it has been since the dawn of time. Happiness means different things to different people but, generally speaking, it is a feeling of contentment, fulfilment, and peace of mind.

Do you understand why it is such an important quality for a mentalist?

We already know that what makes a mentalist so superior is the fact that he can 'connect' to people and become their 'best' friend in a matter of minutes or even seconds!

In order to tap into someone's mind and influence their thoughts and feelings, you must first connect yourself -truly and fully- to that person.

> **Some cause happiness wherever they go; others whenever they go.
> - Oscar Wilde**

No one truly wants to associate with people who constantly project sadness and no one wants to befriend people who are faking happiness. Therefore, before you can connect with anyone else, you must first reach deep down, into the depths of your own soul and discover within yourself what it is that makes you genuinely joyful! Then, once you have unveiled the key to your treasure chest of happiness, you can work on connecting with others and helping them to find their own source of joviality!

Finding your own inner peace will make you a better mentalist. Being relaxed AND happy, will make you a world class mentalist! By achieving both of these personal feats, people will be attracted to you like a magnet, even if you're not a beauty-queen, famous actor or have celebrity status in some other realm. Look around you. Every one of us knows that person, who on the surface is a Plain Jane or less than studly, or even geeky guy; they don't have a "great job", or a lot of money or any particular "social status"; yet, they are often the most popular and compelling people around. Why is that?

Because they have this great spirit, are always smiling and project cheer and merriment wherever they go. One may even go as far as to say they emit an aura that makes them beautiful and alluring to both sexes! This is why it goes to show that it doesn't matter what you look like, as long as you have that secret spark of happiness within you, people will be drawn to you like moths to a flame.

When I teach my students how to master the art of Mentalism and Influence I talk at length about this subject and I will share some of this information here with you.

But before I do, let me tell you some."happy" news: if you focused on my previous lessons and assimilated all the information I shared with you, you now have a good foundation on which to start your search for happiness - you have learned about reducing your stress level through relaxation, and how to achieve a positive attitude. Consider these two skills the stepping-stones which will come together to create your own path to a joy filled life!

A big mistake many people make, and maybe you are one of them, is that they look for bliss in all the wrong places; that is, in the outside world. They depend on other people, events or circumstances to make them happy when, that is not how it works, my friend. True happiness doesn't lie "out there;" it lives within us. But unfortunately, far too many people don't know how to find it inside of themselves. You may ask, "Where inside me is this elusive happiness hiding?"

Well, as we know, "happiness" is not a physical organ like the heart, brain, or liver; rather it is an intangible concept that we cannot see or touch, but we can most definitely feel.

Happiness is a state of mind, and the mind and as you know, can be molded and mended; not literally, of course, but with conscious deliberation and introspection.

So, in essence, the answer to that question actually lies in your own cognitive functions. If your thoughts hold the key to your mood, then having a clear, minimally stressed and focused mind will boost your state of happiness! See how the whole concept of this guide is starting to piece itself together?

Trying to teach someone what makes them happy, using a book, is pretty much impossible. Yes guys, my job isn't easy!

When I used to coach people, it sometimes took months for them to uncover what was necessary to achieve happiness. Yet here, I decided to invite you to try to shortcut the process a bit and attempt to find that happy place within your soul, in order to bring you to the next level.

> **"It isn't what you have, or who you are, or where you are, or what you are doing that makes you happy or unhappy. It is what you think about."**
> *- Dale Carnegie*

Yes, what you think about is key.

You are what you think. Consciously think happy thoughts and you will in turn be happy. Just as the act of smiling triggers an autonomic hormonal reaction in the body that stimulates happiness, a simple thought can accomplish the same thing, without any physical effort at all. A happy mindset is the secret sauce that will make all the steps that I am teaching you in this guide become much easier to perform.

Especially as I mentioned the first step, which is to SMILE. Yes, there is circular reasoning here. Be happy and smile, smile and you will be happy. Win win either way!

I am going to take on a giant feat here, in a small guide. I'm going to try to help YOU figure out the true meaning of happiness in your life. Not the things YOU THINK make you happy, but the things that REALLY make you happy! Please follow the next exercise carefully and give it all the attention it deserves. I promise it can change your life.

I want you to take out a piece of paper and write a list of 20 things that make you happy. They can be anything at all. I do not want to give you boundaries on this first part. To give you a framework it could be - things, people, places, traits, concepts or activities, you get the idea.

How'd it go? Did you do it?

Did you write these 20 things?

Stop right here and don't read any further until you leave this book alone and write that list.

It's crucial.

...

Trust me.

.

.

.

Do it.

.

Don't scroll to the next page before you have written that list.

.

.

Promise?

.

.

Ok.

Once you have completed the list, in writing, flip the page.

I hope you have the list in front of your eyes, because now comes the essence of this exercise: I want you to read the list out loud, one thing after another, and cross off everything that does not have to do with you - specifically you.

For instance, if there is a person that makes you happy, cross them off. If there is a food that makes you happy, cross it off. If there is an object that makes you happy, cross it off.

Now, this does not mean that these things should not make you happy, but rather, I want you to see all of the things that you have listed that had to do with you and only you.

What remains on this list should be a compilation of your traits and hobbies that you, with your own mind and body, without needing anyone else, make up you!

These things are the stepping stones on the path to finding your true happiness in every phase of your life, because they are things of joy that you create for yourself. The only thing in this world that is guaranteed to be forever yours for your whole existence is you.

So since no matter what the circumstances, you will always have you, with you, you can always have happiness with you too.

Some people might finish this exercise and realize that they have crossed off every single thing that they wrote. I know many people who actually have a page with 20 things crossed off at the end. It's ok.

It only means that you need to look deep inside yourself and figure out the true meaning of your own happiness and what that needs in order to blossom.

You might want to try and go back in time, using meditation or the technique of relaxation that I taught you in an earlier lesson, and remember the times you used to laugh so hard that you couldn't control yourself!

Go all the way back, even to the time you were a small child. Try to recollect these memories, and ask yourself what happened in those events that made you so joyous.

By finding the root of the laughter you experienced, you might be able to pinpoint new things that will fill you with cheer.

In my lectures and seminars, I talk in detail about Mindfulness meditation and self-hypnosis; both of which are, in their own unique way, powerful techniques to get in touch with your inner self, gain control over negative thoughts, and create an emotional state you desire which is without a doubt, happiness.

Mindfulness meditation or Shamatha, given its Buddhist origins, is a great tool to achieve tranquillity. It is called "mindful" because it is a conscious process of calming the mind, and an obtainment of self-knowledge achieved through regulated breathing techniques and a continuing state of awareness.

Mindfulness meditation gives you better control over your feelings, and its benefits are numerous. Overall, it allows you to gain improved emotional and physical well-being, which is certainly an important element of happiness.

A mentalist must train his mind to achieve inner peace, serenity and that blissful state we call "happiness." Aside from achieving a total state of relaxation through slow and deep breathing, as I explained previously, happiness involves focusing intently on whatever thoughts, feelings and sensations you experience at that moment.

This is not to say that you will be happy every second of every day; however, eventually and with practice, by using Mindfulness meditation you will reach a blissful state of total calm and serenity while detaching yourself from the problems that have been troubling you and keeping you from finding peace and contentment, overall.

With a clear tranquil mind, you will be best prepared to find the pathway to the mechanisms that trigger your joy.

In recent years, there has been a lot of attention devoted to what actually makes people happy. Modern researchers have uncovered some surprising facts about what "happiness" actually is and what helps us to become happier individuals. Here is a summary of a few of their findings.

See how many of them surprise you or how many of them are currently incorporated within your life:

Discovering who you really are, your life's purpose, your loves and dislikes, in other words, being self-aware, is one of the best ways to increase your happiness.

Social interaction, especially in groups, increases contentment.

Moving your body, whether in team sports, or dancing, or group exercises, ranks up there in reaching high levels of cheer. Solitary exercise is good too - if your body's happy so is your mind.

Being kind to others - philanthropy, altruism, just making a difference in the lives of others, makes a difference in your feelings of self worth, and increases your inner happiness.

Hugging, smiling, which stimulate the production of "happiness" hormones works wonders too. So hug your friends, hug your family, hug your significant others, and hug your pets!

Naturally it follows that having fulfilling relationships in general, boosts your joy.

Try any of these things and see if they work for you. I invite you to find out more ways to find inner happiness, so that you can make the most of your life, find mental and emotional balance, and therefore be the best mentalist, and person, that you can be!

> **"When I was in grade school, they told me to write down what I wanted to be when I grew up. I wrote down happy. They told me I didn't understand the assignment, I told them they didn't understand life.**
> *- John Lennon*

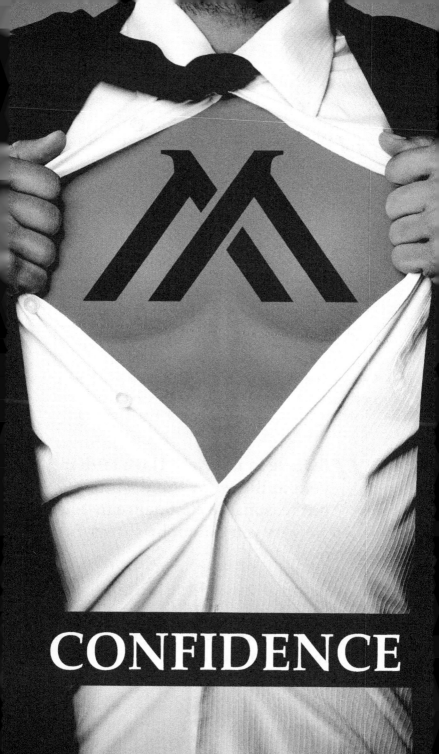

> **With confidence, you have won before you started.**
> *- Marcus Garvey*

STEP 9: CONFIDENCE

This is the spice that builds the Mentalist! You might be wondering: **"Why on earth is confidence such an important quality?"** The answer to that question lies within almost every famous philosopher, thinker, speaker, business-owner and movie star who ever lived. Just listen to what Norman Vincent Peale, one of the gurus of positive thinking said:

> **Believe in yourself! Have faith in your abilities! Without a humble but reasonable confidence in your own powers you cannot be successful or happy.**

or Vince Lombardi who said:

> **Confidence is contagious but so is lack of confidence.**

You have already learned many traits that must be possessed in order to have a positive and influential effect on others. But in order to truly succeed in this new endeavour, it is imperative to be confident in your newfound abilities and powers.

So, the most important question to ask is - do you have confidence in yourself? How high of a regard do you hold your own thoughts, feelings, actions and abilities? If you have to hesitate even a moment, then you do not have enough confidence!

Confidence, put simply, is believing in yourself. As I mentioned in other chapters, being happy as a mentalist is a crucial component to success, however, confidence goes hand in hand with happiness. You need to know you can make yourself happy and you must have the self-assurance to portray that happiness to the world once it is accomplished.

If you have been following along in this guide and have seen enhancement in your mental capabilities through the exercises, congratulations! Not only have you earned personal merit badges on the road to becoming a mentalist, but you have worked hard enough and now know enough to realize that with dedication and perseverance you will be a mentalist; you will have the confidence that you will be able to do anything you set your mind to and influence others to do the same!

It may be a long road, but you can take solace in the fact that you have found a new and exquisite part to yourself. So, bravo!

Take a moment to reflect upon all that you now know you can do, as a result of your dedication to these lessons.

However, I would like to reiterate that everything we do as mentalists should be done not only for the betterment of ourselves, but also in order to help others in any way we can. With that said, I do not want you to confuse being confident with being pompous.

Although your mental prowess, if you continue down the path of becoming a mentalist, will probably surpass the current mental capabilities of your peers, it is important that you do not flaunt this feeling of superiority.

Yes, you have worked hard for all that you have and that you will accomplish, but always remember that we are out to help and progress positivity in our lives and the lives that we touch on a daily basis. There is no shame in being proud of yourself, but others will see your confidence shining through your presence and your capabilities, not your boasts.

Now let us look at another imperative quality of a mentalist; instilling the same kind of confidence they possess, into others they encounter.

Making a person believe in themselves is the best way to persuade them to act in ways constructive for all. My thoughts on the subject can best be summarized by the following words of the great American essayist, lecturer and poet, Ralph Waldo Emerson. Remember them in all your interactions:

"The man of genius inspires us with a boundless confidence in our own powers."

Let's look at an example to show how the above thoughts can play out in real life. What follows is part of an exchange; two different mentalists are trying to influence someone to perform a hard task. I would now like for you to try playing their roles for a second, by reading how each of them says his line:

Mentalist 1: *"Can you do it?"*

Mentalist 2: *"You can do it!"*

Mentalist #1: I'm sure you felt the lack of confidence in the abilities of the target of the statement inherent within the words chosen and phrasing of the question. To be a person capable of persuading, supporting and encouraging another to perform a task, in other words, a REAL mentalist, you must project a sense of genuineness in your belief in another's capabilities.

Obviously the first mentalist's question will not encourage or influence the person he was speaking with into actually performing the task at hand; it will only ignite self-doubt in their heart. They will automatically become consumed in the negative and think: Am I good enough? Strong enough? Fast enough? Smart enough?

Whatever the task might be, you must first exude the belief to a person, that they not only possess all the qualities necessary to perform the feat, but when it is completed, it will have been beneficial and worth the effort. If they are confiding in you about their uneasiness regarding a certain circumstance and their role in it, then they must need something from you that they cannot find within themselves. How can you expect to help someone seeking your support, if you contribute to their sense of insecurity by interjecting your own incertitude into the equation?

Mentalist #2: On the other hand, by putting his words in an affirmative positive statement instead of a question, the second mentalist was infusing his friend with his own confidence in the friend's competency.

The proclamation that the friend "can do it", abolishes the friend's doubts and reaffirms the exact message that his friend truly wants to hear. "You CAN do it!" The bold and genuine pronouncement of this statement leaves no place for question marks, hesitation or scepticism. You can do it. Period.

Confidence in all our transactions is the key to success. Think of all the prominent people like Bill Gates, Warren Buffet, or other high-achievers you know. Do you think any of them would be where they are today if they lacked fortitude and self-belief?

Absolutely, one-hundred percent, without a solitary doubt in my mind, NO! Confidence is the trademark of people we label as extraordinary:

they trust their abilities to think clearly, make good decisions and sound judgments.

They understand who they are and why they were placed on this earth; and, they knew this about themselves way before anyone else did. Most of the time, brilliance and novelty are met with opposition. There is a favorite quote of mine made famous by Apple computers; it has become a kind of mantra for me. Perhaps it will resonate with you too:

"Here's to the crazy ones. The misfits. The rebels. The troublemakers. The round pegs in the square holes. The ones who see things differently. They're not fond of rules. And they have no respect for the status quo. You can quote them, disagree with them, glorify or vilify them. About the only thing you can't do is ignore them; because they change things.

They push the human race forward. And while some may see them as the crazy ones, we see genius. Because the people who are crazy enough to think they can change the world, are the ones who do." There is almost always a time in a prominent person's life where they were either told, or it was inferred, that they could not do what they were confident they could do.

Did you know that Michael Jordan was cut from the varsity basketball team during his sophomore year in high school? Imagine what would have happened if Mr. Jordan internalized and came to believe what his High School coach told him - that he was just not meant to be a basketball player.

He would have given up on his dream, his passion and ultimately the life he was supposed to lead, all because of the opinions of a few short-sighted individuals.

Thankfully, Michael Jordan did not give up on his dream and went on to become one of the most renowned basketball players in the history of the game; and then moved on to even more astonishing feats - providing the world with the iconic movie, Space Jam!

So, are you going to let some high school basketball coach or anyone else in positions of "authority" stand in the way of your dreams, or do YOU have what it takes?

Why should anyone believe in you when you don't even believe in yourself? People will not gravitate towards you if you are unsure of yourself and they certainly will not listen to what you have to say. It may be unfair to be judged so harshly by people who do not really know you, but that is just how it is.

But, let me reiterate-being a powerful mentalist who has confidence in his special skills and abilities doesn't give one the right to be arrogant, conceited, or have a "holier-than-thou" attitude. In the same way that if you fail to exude self-assuredness, there is not a reason in the world anyone should listen to you, hire you, or have a social relationship with you, if you give off a vibe of arrogance people will not want to deal with you either. Arrogant people don't influence others to do anything but turn them off and run the other way.

So you have to temper your self-confident "aura" when dealing with other people. Stand strong in your self-belief while at the same time project a genuinely caring, compassionate and empathetic stance. I know it may feel as though I am drilling this into your head, but this is a super-important concept because this field is all about communication (both verbal and nonverbal), as well as building other people's trust in your, and their abilities.

Being a mentalist is a discipline which requires a great amount of understanding and human connection. If you are not genuine, in any way, shape or form, people will not trust you and although you may be right, people will not listen to you.

In order to get people's attention and incite their interest in what you say or do, you have to project an image of inner strength and exude integrity. How else can you have "mind control" over others, to influence their thoughts and feelings and persuasively guide their actions, when you cannot get them to like, confide and put their faith in you??

Perhaps, this may help; people are afraid of being scammed. People are also afraid to trust anything that they don't understand; and, as I have mentioned before, mentalism is something that very few people without an open mind can grasp. Therefore, if a stranger is even considering asking for your mentalism advice or input and they believe that you faltered, by either having a lack of confidence, or by being showy, then they will fear that you are illegitimate.

You and I may both know that you are a perfectly capable mentalist, able to give that person quality, sound advice, but if that panic switch is flicked on inside their brain, there is little that you can do to turn it off.

So what is the mentalist plan? How can you come across as a confident and secure and likeable person?? I will let you in on a secret known by the advisors of politicians.

Most people will instil faith in someone if they can do two things: look and walk confidently, and be relatable; as they often advise their candidates - come across as someone who people would like as a friend - someone who you can sit down with and have a beer. It is the opinion of many that this is the way George W. Bush won the American Presidency, two times.

He walked and talked with the strength and assuredness of a courageous cowboy, but was affable enough that people could picture themselves having a chat with him over a frosty mug and a bowl full of peanuts. But remember as a mentalist, you must be sort of a chameleon. The famous line "Bait the hook to suit the fish" is very apropos here.

How exactly do you bait the hook? Let's look in greater detail at the best methods. First and foremost you must build the unwaveringly belief in yourself and your abilities, in order to project self confidence; this of course must be coupled with a positive attitude and an optimistic outlook on life. How does one achieve these things?

One of my favorite methodologies for teaching self-improvement, personal development, building your sense of self-worth and bringing you inner peace, is NLP.

Neuro-linguistic programming gives you phenomenal techniques to re-tool the way you were educated and "programmed", as you grew older. Yes, if this sounds like something Bill Gates may say, you are right.

I always explain concepts of the human mind much like one would describe a robot. Our minds are naturally equipped to follow scripts delivered to us by people in "authority"; parents, teachers, bosses, the media - in fact anyone that we look up to, admire or is given respect by ourselves or society.

We have been programmed to "fit" into certain environments - a concept that is perpetuated by all these 'mind controllers'.

They do not all do it on purpose all the time - especially not our parents or teachers, but they believe that "this is the way it is supposed to be"; sometimes, though, it is the way they want us to be, for their own benefit. And unfortunately, too often the result of not "fitting" other people's standards leads to an erosion of self esteem, instead of a celebration of uniqueness.

So, how do you build back the esteem the "controllers" took from you? What is the secret to being "one of those people" who emit confidence in every venture they enter into?

The secret is, like most things, hard work and knowing the basic components that make up a secure individual. Here are a few tips on boosting your self assuredness!

First, truly understand that no one knows everything, but everyone knows something. Repeat this concept to yourself until you are genuinely humble enough to understand that regardless of how good of a mentalist you become, you will never know or be able to know, everything.

Secondly, although the allure of becoming a mentalist may be the excitement of utilizing your mental capabilities to the fullest, letting that go to your head could possibly be your ruin. No matter how seasoned and how sharp of a mentalist you become, sometimes, you will be wrong because you are human. If you can accept that fact and move past it, internalizing what you have learned from a situation, then your confidence will persevere.

On the same note, also remember that everyone has something to teach you. Going back to the beginning of this guide; I spoke about learning everything you can from every moment in your life and every person you meet. Never forget that you can always learn something new from anyone with whom you come in contact. Always be open and willing to accept new thoughts and ideas and never cast off or outright dismiss anyone's outlooks, beliefs, impressions or concepts. Everyone is effectual in some manner and everyone has something to share.

Look at me; I'm a living example of someone who is capable of learning something any time anywhere. Although I perform world-wide, and I spend most of my time in airports and airplanes - flying from one country to another teaching people everywhere these magnificent concepts, and entertaining them in my shows, I am always learning new things! Even in airports!

They're a wonderful place to hone your non-verbal communication, behavior interpretation and prediction skills. People- watching in large crowds can often be the best of all classrooms.

I always read new books and go to other gurus' lectures and seminars; and therefore, my mind is always growing. And the more I come to know, the more I discover that I didn't know. It took me a while to realize what I am about to teach you:

KNOWING you will never KNOW everything there is to KNOW should make you mentally stronger.

Now I understand that you should know 'enough' to want to get better. And after you know 'enough' then you'll want to learn just a 'bit more' to get even a bit better and learn 'some more' to get better and better and so forth. You get the drill!

In the beginning I thought that I couldn't and shouldn't publish this book yet, because I didn't know everything. But now I understand that no one in this world knows everything.

It was thanks to my students who kept asking me to publish this guide that I became more confident in what I did know, so I did published it! And now you're holding it in your hand. Exciting isn't it?

So we see that confidence is something that will never be one hundred percent. You will always have insecurities no matter what. Even people in the most powerful positions in the world have insecurities no matter how confident they appear. So let's repeat my mantra once again:

Knowing you will never know everything there is to know should make you mentally stronger.

And these too are words for reflection:

> **The more you know, the more you realize how much you don't know. The less you know the more you think you know.**
> - *David T. Freeman*

Another piece of advice I have to offer for growing confidence, is to every once and awhile step out of your comfort zone. Take a risk and see which road it leads you down.

If you do not take risks throughout your life, if you become complacent, then your level of confidence also becomes static. You need to break that cycle of existing in total comfort, to learn. Becoming a mentalist is all about testing the boundaries of your mind.

As long as you are living, there are still boundaries to be pushed, experiences to be had and, yes, mistakes to be made. The more you push yourself, the more you will accomplish.

The more you accomplish, the greater your level of confidence will be and soon, although you may be nervous, you will constantly crave the opportunity for something new. That craving is another sign of your inner strength, so embrace it.

Even if you try and do not succeed at something, it is still a lesson learned. As Thomas Edison said in response to his alleged failure to create the light bulb, thus far, "I have not failed. I've just found a thousand ways that won't work"; meaning, that he has learned a thousand new things through a thousand different experiences!

In an effort to step out of your comfort zone without really taking a gigantic leap (baby steps are always the key to trying new things), change something small in your daily routine and build from there. For instance, sit at a different spot at the dinner table, write with the opposite hand or ask a stranger on a date.

It takes small steps to eventually climb mountains, so take it slowly; but, definitely try to do something that you are not at ease with in order to get your self esteem ball rolling!

Remember that Bill Gates, Michael Jordan, Winston Churchill, the President of the United States and every other huge influencer you can come up with has had their moments of insecurities.

And if they can be giant successes, despite the fact they aren't 100% confident 100% of the time - **YOU CAN DO IT TOO!**

I also want to make you aware that a huge confidence builder is to practice depersonalizing the criticism you receive. Are you going to make mistakes? Yes. You are human and you will always be human and as such, you will always make mistakes. However, it is how you deal with those mistakes that reinforce your confidence and mental faculties. It is human nature for someone to take criticism as a personal attack. Sometimes, given the circumstance, it is almost easier to characterize the criticism as a personal attack.

However, despite the circumstance or the criticism, it is always better to depersonalize the person's comments. Even if you truly feel the criticism is a personal attack, take solace in the fact that everyone is entitled to his opinion. Think about what they say, determine whether you can find merit in anything in it and once you have extracted all useful information, toss the remains out of your mind. There is no room in one's mind for negativity -retain the positive benefit of having learned something from it.

Granted, this is not an easy thing to do, and even as you become a better mentalist and influence more and more people in your daily life - there may still be comments that make you feel as if you were personally called out; but just focus on the learning aspect of it - even if you can't derive anything positive from the content of the comment itself.

Perhaps you can learn something about the behavior of the person who made the comment. Just try to disregard any personal angst against that person and refrain from retaining any negative feelings about yourself that may have been stirred up within you.

As a mentalist, you will know yourself better than anyone. You will have a reason for why you do anything. You know the extent of your abilities and you know what you are and are not capable of doing. Again, just like the example of Michael Jordan and his high school basketball coaches, if he had taken their criticism to heart and allowed them to rule the extent of his talent, you probably would never have heard of Michael Jordan, the world renowned basketball player.

You must also remember to be aware of your own body language and know how to send out and control non-verbal signals. Certain facial expressions, gestures, and body positions will speak louder than words. You can tell people "I am confident," but if you don't look them straight in the eye and you sit in a hunched position, they will see you as just the opposite – insecure and unsure of yourself. But, if you gaze right at them, give a firm handshake, and sit (or stand) straight, they will perceive you as self-assured.

As a professional mentalist you'll need to follow all the steps outlined in this book. These techniques are very effective in turning negative and self-defeating thoughts into empowering ones. The more you practice these steps, the more confident you will become.

You can increase your confidence by increasing your ego, self-esteem and self-image. Ego and egotism have received a bashing in the media with celebrities often labeled as having misguided or inflated egos. However, building your ego to a strong and healthy amount should not be thought of as a negative thing.

Everyone needs to have a certain level of ego within themselves to function properly; otherwise, they would not be able to adequately interact and be a contributing social member of society - able to share and exchange thoughts, ideas and concepts.

So how can you increase your ego, self esteem and self-image? By the methods I have previously outlined, and by practicing the following succinct script which will enable you to increase your confidence dramatically. It takes the form of self-affirmations. An affirmation is a "statement or proposition that is declared to be true."

The theory behind affirmations is that when there is a perceived threat to self-image, it can be bolstered again by repetitively re-confirming confidence in other areas.

It is based upon the belief that the more you repeat something the better you will learn it, and/or believe it; so by transference, the more you repeat these affirmations the more you will begin to believe them. For simplicity, I have embedded them within an ego-strengthening script but you can also formulate your own without much difficulty.

For example, if you want to become a happier person you could say:

> *'Each and every day, in every way, I am becoming happier and happier.'*

After a small amount of time, you will begin to accept this as true, and therefore it will be true. As you work towards your life goals, you do become happier and happier with every passing day. Construct your own affirmations in a little notebook and repeat them at the start of each day, perhaps when you have your breakfast, and notice how quickly they can have a highly positive affect on your life.

Confidence building affirmations

- *I am self-reliant, self-confident and filled with independence and determination.*
- *I have opened my mind to the inner security that was lying dormant within me.*
- *I am transformed.*
- *I am self-confident.*
- *I think confidently, I talk confidently, and I project an image of self-confidence.*
- *I am independent and filled with inner security.*
- *I am self-confident internally and externally.*
- *My inner confidence has emerged.*
- *I am creating a new positive reality.*

- *I now experience all the warmth and joy in life while detaching from negativity.*

- *From this moment on I see the positive side of everything that happens in my life.*

- *I see positive opportunities in everything I experience.*

- *My positive thinking now results in a more positive life.*

- *I experience a feeling of overall well-being and mental calm.*

- *I am at peace with myself, the world, and everyone in it.*

- *Each and every day I experience more and more positive results of my positive thinking.*

- *My self-esteem is increasing.*

- *My self-confidence is increasing.*

- *I feel enthusiastic about my life and look forward to the challenges.*

- *I now breathe life with new optimism . with new enthusiasm.*

- *A happy, self-assured inner me has emerged.*

- *I am a positive individual who sees problems only as opportunities.*

- *I am patient, calm and harmoniously centered at all times.*

- *I let go of all fear-based emotions such as blame, jealousy, guilt, anger and possessiveness.*

- *Negative emotions are now part of my past and I use them only as building blocks for a more positive future.*

- *I am independent and self-responsible and I fully realize that I am unlimited in my ability to create my own reality.*

- *I keep my mind like calm water.*

- *I remain centered at all times; this means to be physically relaxed, emotionally calm, mentally focused and alert.*

- *I am confident and secure about everything.*

- *I maintain a calm mind and think only positive thoughts.*

- *I no longer worry about things I cannot change.*

- *I am confident, secure and mentally at peace.*

With a little bit of practice, these affirmations, and the affirmations which you create for yourself can come to govern your life and how you see yourself.

You can become the driving force behind your own confident life and choose who you want to be.

FINAL WORDS

I hope you've enjoyed the ride! Before I come to a close, I would like to take a moment to reiterate what has been learned. I believe it is not only important for something to be explained, but then restated, in order to bring to light things that might have been missed. Once you become a seasoned mentalizer, there will be few details that you will miss, however for the time being, I feel that it is only fair to recap once more.

In the first lesson, we spoke about **Smiling** and how that is important for your overall attractability to other people. You must smile in order to be approachable.

If you smile genuinely, your essence glows and invites people to acknowledge you, appreciate your presence, listen and open up to you.

There is nothing that a killer smile cannot overcome. Smiling is the universal language, and is an emotional contagion, so make sure that you learn it and use it constantly in influencing everyone you meet!

During the second lesson, we talked about **Listening**. Remember, we stressed not only hearing what the person has to say on a superficial level, but listening intently with only the purpose of hearing the content of their answer and the intonation of the delivery.

While actively listening you must keep all of your attention on them; observing their words as well as the tone and pitch of their voice. Notice their body language and whether they keep eye contact with you - which is crucial to actively listening and getting the whole story - this means internalizing the silent communications, those that were verbally never said.

The third lesson spoke about **Focus**. A large part of being a successful mentalist is being able to shut everything else off and studying one thing in particular at a time and everything at one time. This lesson expounded on lesson two. Instead of just listening to the person you are talking to, you must also focus entirely on them.

There is nothing that should be distracting you from everything they are doing; not even thinking about what you should say to them in responsive dialogue, which again, is a common Active listening mistake.

If you are really paying attention and focusing entirely on the person you are speaking to, then the right words will come when they are needed.

If you are truly focusing, you will not only intuitively know far more than they are telling you, but you will also invite them to tell you more, even if you do not say a thing.

Sometimes, it is just better to listen than to speak because then, once you do have a question, it will be one of far more depth than anything you could have concocted simply because you were trying to ask a question to show that you were indeed listening.

In the **fourth lesson**, the theme was being **Understanding and having empathy**. I went over the kind of questions you should ask in order to receive more responsive and thorough answers than just "yes" and "no", or an equivalent. For someone who wants to influence people, gaining information from what people tell you is an important part of getting a feel for who they are, in the quickest amount of time.

If you are trying to help someone, but must first ask them for a detailed report of their life since birth, you've entered a situation that can produce too much extraneous information, will be very intrusive and will waste a lot of precious time.

If you remember, in the **fifth lesson**, we went over the need to have a **good Memory**. A good memory is important because it allows you to internalize and process all that you have observed.

With a good memory, even things that seemed unimportant at the time are filed away in a mentalists' Working and Long Term memory, but can be called upon at any moment when that detail becomes important. It is just another way how you as a mentalist, as well as your brain's mental capabilities, are truly awe-inspiring!

In addition, there are plenty of ways on how to increase and sharpen the capabilities of your memory. Regardless of how long you have been practicing with and expanding your mental faculties, there is never a limit on how far you can enhance, expand and sharpen your memory; it is only a matter of putting in the time to do so.

But since you will always see results, you will be motivated to challenge every part of yourself all the time; so that will not be a problem!

During the **sixth lesson**, I stressed the need to be **Relaxed**. As hard as you work at expanding your mental capabilities, you must also allow them time to rest - which expands beyond the time that you have extended periods of sleep.

Sleep is all well and good, but in order to achieve the goals you have set for yourself as a mentalist, you must also allow yourself some conscious down-time. A great, proven stress reliever is meditation. As we discussed, mediation can come in many forms and can be done for many different lengths of time and still be successful. Therefore, the question should not be "for how long should I practice meditation", but rather, "how can I fit meditation into my lifestyle."

If you make time for relaxation in your everyday life, you will see that your work ethic, positivity and all-around disposition will change dramatically for the better - making you happier and excited to face the day ahead!

The **seventh lesson** spoke about **Attitude** and how your mindset and mental outlook will automatically affect the course of your day.

Fortunately, if you genuinely portray a pleasant attitude, which encompasses all of the other lessons we have learned thus far, people will find you more approachable and will be more apt to listen to what you have to say.

Having a good attitude first thing in the morning, every morning will get your day started off on the right foot, and in addition to it, attract the attention of others who will be completely influenced by it; this in turn, will have a positive inward affect on you. Having a positive attitude will lead to a better overall perception of yourself, it will make you happier and far more inclined to tackle whatever tasks the day has in store for you!

In the **eighth lesson**, finding **Peace and Happiness** was discussed. Once you find you happiness, inner peace will follow.

Having inner peace and happiness is essential to anyone who desires to touch other people because, like other forms of positivity, once you find inner peace it will emit from you, influencing everyone you come into contact with. Therefore, people will be naturally drawn to you with the hope of finding their own inner peace and happiness, which will allow you the opportunity to help them.

It is all about being approachable, and if you are outwardly happy and at peace with yourself, then you are automatically approachable!

The **ninth and final lesson** of this guide is to have **Confidence** in everything you do! By having confidence, you will be magnetic and captivate people, making them feel more comfortable taking your advice and direction.

You will be comforted in the fact that you are aware of who you are, and what you stand for; this is the cornerstone of being a good mentalist.

You do not have to be pretentious or arrogant in displaying a confident demeanor; you just have to be sure in your stance - others will naturally pick up on it without you saying anything overt.

People who are said to have a "presence" exude confidence from their entire being; others are drawn to such people who may do nothing else but simply walk into a room. Confidence is alluring; if you have got it, everyone will know it!

These are all very simple avenues to sharpen your mental powers, and if you learn and practice all these skills in your daily life, you'll be amazed at how much keener, more alert and more analytical your mind will become.

I will stop and say that although the actions behind these steps are simple to take, the ideas behind them are phenomenal. If I would meet you at the corner of a street and tell you that you would be able to influence people merely by smiling, listening, focusing and understanding them, you would probably say something like "NO WAY!"

This is why I had to write an entire book about these ideas; and explain in detail, the mentalism theories that each step involve. And there you have it! It is simple in practice, but not AS simple in theory. You must understand the entire psychology behind each step and how to approach it from a mentalist point of view.

After perfecting these steps, and putting them into practice, there may be those who witness your displays and exclaim that you have developed "Superpowers"!

Having superpowers does not mean that you will be able to fly like Superman or leap from tall buildings like Spider-man; obviously that is fictional.

However, even if your abilities are perceived in a superpower like manner, I urge you NOT to test your newfound capabilities like that! These powers reside in your mind and can be expanded with curiosity and knowledge, not through physical exertion and the defiance of gravity!

Do I want you to push yourself in order to strengthen your mental acuity, yes! Absolutely! Although, since these abilities are strictly mental, thinking of them in the wrong way could mess with your head, literally; and end up causing more harm than good.

Once you become a very good mentalist, you will feel the possibilities flowing through your mind every moment of every day; however, if you are allow the internal power to overtake you, it will only lead to hurting people's feelings and perhaps, others fearing you.

So, in keeping with the Spiderman theme, Peter's uncle told him, "With great power comes great responsibility." This is true, even for those who do not fly or leap from tall buildings, so take care with the potent faculties that you will possess.

This reminds me of a childhood experience I had as a little mentalist kid. I used to know so many things about so many people that when my friend Karen asked me once: **"Ehud, how do you know**

all these things? Do you have SUPERNATURAL POWERS?" I simply replied: **"My powers are so natural, it's super!"**

Being a mentalist is exactly what it is. There are no "powers", no hidden doors and no tricks; it just is what it is. You see, people as a whole have gotten so far away from nature in our generation, that we stopped 'listening' to the language of the universe. We have stopped paying attention to all of the signals out there that are meant to give us guidance.

The earth and everything that surrounds us, from the inner-workings of gravity to the stars shining in the night sky, have survived for millions of years! How, in all of that time, could it not have an exuberant amount of eminent and relevant knowledge to impart to us? How can it not have real, tangible answers to reveal to us?

However, our society, the world over, either thinks that they know better, or they simply do not care about those lessons and, thus, they have ignored this knowledge for so long, that most do not even realize that this intelligence is out there and attainable. It is for this reason that I believe becoming a mentalist should be something you learn in school as a child.

Our minds have dulled, thanks to less of a threat to our survival; we have become complacent mentally, as well as in our lives. Becoming a mentalist will return that intuitive sense that humans were always meant to possess and enhance our daily lives.

Although we may not need to use our mental capability for survival on a daily bases, becoming a mentalist will bring us back to who we once were: beings who are attuned to nature and everything around them.

If you have been following this guide correctly and taking it step by step, I know that you have noticed a difference in yourself already! But remember- practice, practice, practice. If you don't apply what you have learned here at every opportunity, you will soon forget the principles. They must become habit - ingrained into your very being.

The great Bernard Shaw, famous essayist, novelist, playwright etc. and co-founder of the London School of Economics once said:

> **If you teach a man anything, he will never learn."**

Dale Carnegie, the motivational writer, furthered the thought stating:

> **Shaw was right. Learning is an active process. We learn by doing. you are not merely trying to learn information; you are attempting to form new habits, which take time, persistence, patience and daily application. Only knowledge that is used sticks in your mind."**

"

So as I conclude here, remember the words of these great men.

Become what you do.

Incorporate these skills into your life, until they become you.

If you take the advice given in this guide, you will be well on your way to becoming not only a mentalist and a great influencer, communicator and persuader, but also the best version of yourself possible; the one that you were always meant to be!

Good luck!

Ehud Segev

FOR MORE INFORMATION ABOUT EHUD SEGEV AND MENTALIZER EDUCATION VISIT MENTALIZER.COM

Made in the USA
Monee, IL
16 November 2020